ISAAC HALEVY

(1847-1914)

ISAAC HALEVY

ISAAC HALEVY

(1847-1914)

Spokesman and Historian
of Jewish Tradition

by

RABBI O. ASHER REICHEL, D.H.L.

YESHIVA UNIVERSITY PRESS
NEW YORK, 1969

© 1969 O. ASHER REICHEL

Library of Congress Catalog Card No. 70-85704

Printed in the United States of America by
BALSHON PRINTING & OFFSET CO.

Table of Contents

Foreword

The Hebrew saying, "It is easier to be a critic than to be creative," has often been used to characterize Halevy's contributions to Jewish historiography and Jewish history. The tag which was attached to this giant scholar and researcher is often unfair and more often unjust. True, in his monumental work, *Dorot Harishonim,* he carries on a polemic with his enlightened predecessors, such as Frankel, Geiger, Graetz and many others. But this does not necessarily postulate that his ingenuity consisted primarily in being a "nein zoger." One may venture to say that had Halevy lived prior to the great men of the Haskalah movement, with whom he often vehemently disagreed, but whose opinions he respected at times, he would have occupied even a greater place as a historian.

In fact, his penetrating interpretations and conceptual understanding of original Jewish sources, particularly Talmudic, would have helped historians who preceded him, to write Jewish history with greater profundity; and they would have avoided their unintentional mistakes in judgment. His definitions of the disagreements between the Sadducees and Pharisees are still indispensible for the Jewish historian as a source material. If historians before his days had understood the underpinnings of the many halakhic differences between the schools of Shamai and Hillel, they would not have made as many mistakes in presenting a Jewish point of view to a non-Jewish world, particularly in matters of marriage and divorce.

Halevy not only wrote history but also pioneered in the making of Jewish history in his contemporary religious environment. This unknown phase of Halevy's life is exceptionally well presented by the author, using published and unpublished correspondence which appear in this volume.

It therefore affords me great satisfaction to congratulate Rabbi Reichel for "resurrecting" a great Jewish scholar who almost became the "forgotten man."

I have known Dr. Reichel both as a brilliant former Talmudic student of mine and later, as a friend and colleague. Indeed, very few, if any, are as intellectually equipped and spiritually attuned as he is to give an evaluation of the immortal Rabbi Isaac Halevy Rabinowitz. I recall that since his boyhood the author has had two great mentors: Rabbi Samson Raphael Hirsch and Rabbi Isaac Halevy Rabinowitz, the two men who influenced Jewish thinking and living for centuries to come.

In this book Rabbi Reichel with intellectual honesty, rabbinic knowledge and above all, compassionate affinity, evaluates Halevy in his many facets as a man, as a highly respected Talmudic lay scholar, historiographer, and the moving spirit and one of the founders of Agudath Israel.

I recommend this book highly to laymen and scholars alike.

With Torah greetings,

SAMUEL BELKIN
President
Yeshiva University

February, 1969

Preface

THE HISTORY OF Orthodox Judaism at the turn of the twentieth century has been deeply enriched by the indelible imprint of Rabbi Yitzhak Isaac Halevy (Rabinowitz). Yet he is virtually unknown in our day.

Halevy's magnum opus on Jewish history, *Dorot Harishonim* (Generations of Yore), spans the Biblical, Talmudic, and Gaonic eras. In that work — the first volume was published in 1897 and the sixth in 1964 — the fundamentals of Jewish tradition were reaffirmed. This aspect of Halevy's accomplishments spearheaded a religiously-oriented Jewish scholarship as well as the development of the *Juedisch-Literarische Gesellschaft* in 1901 and its subsequent publications.

It was also Halevy's role as the master architect and self-sacrificing pioneer in championing Orthodox Judaism in modern times that was instrumental in the founding in 1912 of Agudath Israel, a world-wide religious movement. However, he has not been given due recognition as a founding father of the Agudath Israel, nor has his imprint upon religious education in the Holy Land under the aegis of the *Freie Vereinigung* in Germany been adequately recorded for posterity.

Halevy made his mark in two different worlds — in the leading rabbinical circles in Russia in the second half of the nineteenth century, and among the Orthodox leadership in Germany from 1900 until his death in Hamburg in 1914. What makes Halevy's life story unique is that his august reputation among the Talmudic-centered rabbis of Russia blended with his scholarly pursuits and communal endeavors in West European circles.

9

Although Halevy lived into this century (I have been in contact with some of his contemporaries), the bulk of the source materials relating to Halevy's activities were either lost or destroyed in Europe during the holocaust of World War II. Thus in 1948 when I interviewed Jacob Rosenheim, president of the Agudath Israel World Organization, he did not possess even one letter of more than a thousand he had received from Halevy dealing with every detail of the Agudah's development from 1908 until Halevy's death. As for the archives of the *Freie Vereinigung,* Dr. Salomon Ehrman of Zurich ruefully informed me that nothing of significance remained. Halevy's family, resident in Israel, likewise could not contribute any biographical data. One grandson wrote, "Even to us very little is known about our grandfather's life."

Fortunately, Halevy's lasting achievements and influences beyond his creative pen and casual references in encyclopedias can now be presented in some measure thanks to a collection of his heretofore unpublished correspondence that has come to light.

In the course of my graduate studies it was brought to my attention that a collection of Halevy correspondence was for sale. I lost no time in purchasing these original letters, along with some copies and drafts, numbering about 175 items. One hundred and twenty-five letters were addressed to Halevy's close friend, Dr. Heimann Kottek, the Rabbi of Bad Homburg, near Frankfurt. These were dated from 1905 to 1912, when Kottek died. The others were written in the 1900's (except for one in 1897) to such rabbinical luminaries as Salomon Breuer, Haim Ozer Grodzensky, Abraham I. Kook, Shalom Duber Schneersohn (of Liubavich) and Haim Soloveichik, as well as to Wolf Jawitz, Jacob Rosenheim, and Halevy's son, Samuel. Many of the figures involved in the Halevy correspondence are listed in various encyclopedias.

From his early days Halevy was in the forefront of literary and communal skirmishes with forces that he considered inimical to Orthodox Judaism. Likewise in his correspondence Halevy did not hesitate to express his forthright opinions concerning ideas, events, and personalities. Since all of his correspondence was interwoven with subjects of immediate purpose and concern to him, the reader of his letters may discern at close range his dynamic, creative thinking, as well as a composite of his towering personality. Many of these letters likewise afford intimate glimpses of his thoughts and activities. Thus Halevy's life as recorded by his own hand *in medias res* revealed many facets of his personality that no other person, not even his closest associates, could possible portray.

Since Halevy's pen was the major means of communicating the events in which he played key roles, the observation of Thomas Jefferson is significant here: "The letters of a person, especially of one whose business had been chiefly transacted by letters, form the only full and genuine journal of his life." The Halevy correspondence, with its extensive bearing on his communal activities and his views on Jewish scholarship, must indeed also be considered an integral part of his writings in Jewish history and Jewish thought.

The portrayal of the dynamic life of Halevy within the covers of this volume likewise brings to the fore some interesting facets of the history of Jewish life in Europe and in the Holy Land from the 1870's to 1914.

Halevy's historic accomplishments as defender of his people's spiritual heritage on the intellectual as well as communal battle fronts in the last two decades of his life were attained in the face of great personal misfortune. Yet until his dying day his mantle of faith and righteousness clung to him as steadfastly as during the days of his youthful enthusiasm. His life and works have proved him worthy of the title, Prince in Israel.

New York, 5729   O. A. R.

Acknowledgments

This volume is an extensive revision of my doctoral dissertation, *The Life and Letters of Rabbi Isaac Halevy* (1847-1914), submitted to the Bernard Revel Graduate School of Yeshiva University. It followed the writing of my M.H.L. thesis, *Isaac Halevy's Evaluation of Sadduceeism,* at the Harry Fischel School of Higher Jewish Studies of Yeshiva University.

I wish to express my profound gratitude to my faculty sponsors at the Yeshiva University, Prof. Sidney B. Hoenig in whose Jewish History class at Yeshiva College I first learned of Halevy, and who has been a constant mentor in the scholarly aspects and preparation of this work; and to Prof. Isaac Lewin for his constructive suggestions. I likewise record with reverence my debt to the late Prof. Samuel K. Mirsky for his learned guidance.

I am most grateful to the Trustees of the Harry and Jane Fischel Foundation for making possible the publication of this work. When Harry Fischel, of blessed memory, the grandfather of my beloved wife, left these shores to settle in the Holy Land in 1947, I had asked him to help me in my search for Halevy source materials. In his first letter to me from Jerusalem, he referred to his efforts in this regard.

I also wish to thank the following who have been helpful in many ways: Mr. William Aron, Dr. Moses Auerbach, Rabbi Philip Biberfeld, Rabbi Joseph Breuer, Rabbi and Mrs. Shear-Yashuv Cohen, Prof. Jacob I. Dienstag, Dr. Markus Elias, Rabbi Herbert S. Goldstein, Dr. Edward I. Kiev, Mr. Lawrence Kobrin, Dr. Shelly P. Koenigsberg, Dr. Fred Koffler, Dr. Bernard Lander, my dear children, Aaron, Miriam, and Hillel, and the staff members of the libraries of the Jewish Institute of Religion, the New York Public Library, Yeshiva University and Yivo.

Veaharon, aharon havivah — were it not for the superhuman devotion, patience, and constant assistance of my devoted wife, Josephine Hannah, in the preparation of every page, this work would have been only an unrealized vision.

Introductory Notes

The entire collection of Halevy letters along with the Hebrew edition of this biography of Rabbi Isaac Halevy is being published by the Mosad Harav Kook in Jerusalem entitled *Rabbi Yitzhak Isaac Halevy — Hayav Veigrotav.* In the Hebrew edition the Halevy correspondence appears in chronological order. References to the Halevy letters in this work are cited in the footnotes with the preface, "Halevy Number."

The calligraphy of the Halevy correspondence is so impressive that it is deemed worthy of reproduction. Accordingly, a selection of Halevy's original letters are included in the Appendix of this volume.

CHAPTER ONE

Ivenec, Vilna and Volozhin (1847-1895)

YITZHAK ISAAC HALEVY RABINOWITZ was born into a distinguished rabbinical family on the eleventh of Tishrei, 5608 (1847), in Ivenec, Province of Minsk, near Vilna. He was a scion of the "renowned Ivenec family in Russia,"[1] whose lineage was traced back for generations.[2]

Halevy was named after R. Isaac Ivenecer who was financially instrumental in the founding of the Volozhin Yeshiva in 1804 with R. Haim, a disciple of the Gaon of Vilna.[3] R. Isaac Ivenecer's father, R. Eliyahu, counted among his possessions the village of Kamin near Ivenec. R. Isaac's son, R. Lippelle Ivenecer, was the son-in-law of the illustrious R. Samuel ben Avigdor (died 1791), the last to hold the title of *Av Bet Din* of Vilna.[4] It was in an atmosphere of learning, piety and affluence that R. Nahum Haim, the son-in-law of R. Lippelle, held his grandson, Yitzhak Isaac, on his knees.

Halevy's mother, Rahel, was the daughter of R. Mordecai Eliezer Kovner[5] of Vilna, who was financially independent and devoted virtually all of his time to Torah study. He was the

[1] Inscribed on Halevy's tombstone — see below p. 159.

[2] Benjamin Rivlin, "*Ilan Hayahas*," *Sefer Zikaron Lerabbee Yitzhak Isaac Halevy*, pp. 74-79.

[3] Samuel Halevy, "*Avee Zikhrono Livrakhah*," *Sefer Zikaron Lerabbee Yitzhak Isaac Halevy*, pp. 13-15.

[4] The title *Moreh Zedek* was substituted until after World War I. Israel Cohen, "The Chief Rabbis of Vilna," *Essays Presented to J. H. Hertz*, (London, 1942), pp. 90-94.

H. N. Maggid noted in his *Ir Vilna*, p. 17, that Halevy had shown him the manuscript of R. Samuel's first sermon.

[5] He is listed in *op. cit.*, p. 253.

15

author of *Karnei Re'em* and comments on Tractate *Shabbat* which were published in the Vilna edition of the Talmud in 5645.

Halevy's father, R. Eliyahu, was in his twenties when he was accidentally killed by soldiers in his home. Thus it came about that Halevy's grandfather, R. Nahum Haim, raised him like a son and they became very attached to each other.

When Halevy was still a child, his home town, Ivenec, was destroyed by fire, an occurrence not uncommon in those days — which brought about the dispersal of his family. Halevy was taken to Minsk and afterwards to the home of his maternal grandfather, R. Mordecai Eliezer Kovner, in Vilna.

At the age of six, Halevy was already studying Talmud. When he was thirteen years old he entered the Volozhin Yeshiva where he became known as a Talmudic prodigy and a favorite of R. Joseph Duber Soloveichik. After a year's stay at the Yeshiva, Halevy returned to Vilna where he continued to study on his own. In later years R. Joseph Duber addressed him in his correspondence, as "Beloved of God, beloved of my soul, and beloved of all men."

When he was eighteen years old Halevy married Elke, the daughter of his uncle, R. Saul Kovner,[6] of Kovno. He was offered a rabbinical post in a city near Minsk but his wife and other members of the family dissuaded him — a decision he always regretted. The tea business which was mainly conducted by his wife afforded him time for his communal activities as well as for the continuation of his studies late into the night.

It was his custom upon returning from the morning *minyan* to devote the first two hours of the day to his writings; afterward he turned to his correspondence and then to his business. Beginning with his younger days he spent each Friday in the

---

[6] *Ibid.,* p. 254.

study of the *Mishneh Lamelekh*[7] and the *Noda Beyehudah*[8] for an uninterrupted six hour period. In later years he referred to these two works as his master instructors.

Among his early writings was a commentary on the Talmud entitled, *Battim Levaddim*.[9] At the time of his passing it was still in manuscript form.[10]

It did not take long before Halevy assumed a prominent role in rabbinical circles in Russia. The Vilna community appointed him *menahel* (director) of the Ramaila's Yeshiva[11] where he later became the head *menahel*.[12] At the age of twenty-one he was signally honored by the famed Volozhin Yeshiva with the designation of *gabbai* (warden). He was awarded this elevated appointment although he was rather young — few dignitaries of the Jewish community were so honored — in recognition of his efforts in resolving satisfactorily a dispute between the head of the Yeshiva, R. Naphtali Z. J. Berlin, and the widow of the former head, R. Eliezer Yitzhak Fried, when many older rabbis were unable to be of help.[13]

Halevy's unique role in the Yeshiva's administration was aptly evaluated by the famed R. Haim Soloveichik years later when he remarked to a circle of old acquaintances, "There was only *one gabbai* in Volozhin — R. Yitzhak Isaac!"[14] Halevy's son recalled in the biography of his father that on one occasion when his father was unable to attend a meeting of the leaders of the Volozhin Yeshiva which was convened in Minsk, they

---

[7] Commentary on the *Mishneh Torah* of Maimonides.

[8] By R. Ezekiel Landau.

[9] From Exodus XXV:27.

[10] Inscribed on his tombstone. See below p. 28.

[11] Or "Reb Maila's," founded in 1831. See I. Cohen, *Vilna*, p. 269.

[12] E. A. Rabinowitz, *"Haval al Deavdin,"* *Hamodia*, 26 Iyar 5674, p. 466.

[13] "Rabbi Jischok Halevy," *Der Israelit*, May 23, 1929, p. 1.

M. Berlin, *Fun Volozhin Biz Yerushalayim*, p. 109, listed Halevy among the *gabboim* of the Yeshiva. He also related an episode on p. 105 alluding to Halevy in his role as *gabbai* without mentioning him by name.

[14] S. Halevy, *op. cit.*, p. 18.

telegraphed him that without his participation the meeting would not take place. Moved by their plea, he made a special trip from Vilna.

In the wake of Halevy's appointment as *gabbai* at the Volozhin Yeshiva, his reputation as a leading rabbinical personality was well established. Rabbis and laymen alike leaned heavily upon his judicious advice. From his modest study in Vilna Halevy would come forward with the necessary strategy for the defense of the Torah.

In 1872 a Commission on Jewish Affairs appointed by the Russian Government was ready to submit its report. Halevy, who was twenty-five years old at the time, composed letters to the influential Baron Joseph Yozel Guenzburg and to his son, Baron Horace, of St. Petersburg, on behalf of the religious community, urging them to be on the Commission.[15]

Halevy participated in the major conferences that took place in the home of R. Isaac Elchanan Spektor of Kovno (Kovno was three hours from Vilna by train). Halevy was often delegated to carry out the decisions of the conferences.

On one occasion, when Halevy came to a large conference in Vilna, one of the elders remarked, "Welcome, R. Isaac...We were awaiting you as we could not come to any decision before your arrival."

Halevy's intense interest in the Holy Land was also evidenced in his early years. *Etrogim* were the major export of the Holy Land and a vital factor in its economy. When the *etrogim* from the Holy Land could not compete with the *etrogim* that were imported from the Greek island of Corfu, Halevy was instrumental in having R. Isaac Elchanan of Kovno ban the Corfu *etrogim*.[16] Subsequently the Corfu *etrogim* were removed from the open market in all of Russia.

---

[15] *Ibid.*, pp. 19-21. A Halevy letter to Baron Horace Guenzburg is quoted *loc cit.*
[16] *Der Israelit*, June 6, 1929, p. 1.

In Czarist Russia the status of the Jews depended in large measure upon their subtle intercessions with the government officials. Inasmuch as Vilna was the capital district of Greater Lithuania as well as the center of religious Jewry, the decisions of the Ministry of Education in St. Petersburg affecting Jewish education in particular, were based mainly upon the reports and replies to the questionnaires emanating from Vilna. Halevy's personality and intellect impressed the Russian official, Smirnoff, who was the director of the Ministry of Education in Vilna. Smirnoff visited his home frequently to discuss at length with him matters of contemporary interest. Halevy's views were eagerly sought by him especially on matters relating to the Government's involvement in the Yeshivos and *hadarim* (elementary religious schools). In due time, Smirnoff's reports and recommendations were dispatched to St. Petersburg only after he had consulted Halevy. Thus with Halevy's guidance Smirnoff succeeded in counteracting many of the well laid plans of the *maskilim* (adherents of the enlightenment movement), whose aim was to destroy the prevailing religious educational structure.[17]

In the early 1880's the Volozhin Yeshiva was about to be closed down by the government as a result of the relentless efforts of the *maskilim*. It was Smirnoff's intervention with the Ministry of Education under the direction of Halevy that staved off the decree. Though Halevy carried the burden of Volozhin on his shoulders, his actions were not publicized. Notwithstanding all his efforts, however, Halevy witnessed the closing of the Yeshiva in 1892. Though reopened shortly thereafter, it never regained its former glory. This distressing experience undoubtedly contributed to the militancy in his writings against the antitraditional elements.

[17] S. Halevy, *op. cit.*, pp. 23 ff.; *Der Israelit, ibid.*, p. 2.
J. Lipschitz (*Zikhron Yaakov*, III, p. 143) refers to a Sergeyevsky in a similar role.

In 1892 the Russian Government decreed that the head
melamed (teacher) of each *heder* would have to pass an
examination for certification which would require a background of secular studies. It was evident that the entire
system of *hadarim* was imperiled since the Government
knew that the *melamdim* could not meet these requirements.
The Ministry of Education in St. Petersburg sent a lengthy
questionnaire to Smirnoff, its director in Vilna, relating to this
matter. Were he to have replied in accordance with the Ministry's
standards, the entire structure of Jewish education in Russia
would have been in jeopardy. However, Halevy helped Smirnoff
formulate his report so that the *hadarim* were for the first time
officially sanctioned.

Some time later, Smirnoff, crestfallen, reported to Halevy that
all their efforts had been in vain because the government had
ordered that all the *melamdim* would henceforth be required to
have their photographs attached to their teaching certificates —
something which he thought the *melamdim* would refuse to do.
Halevy pointed out that the accepted custom of shunning photographs was not a basic prohibition. In this instance the verse in
Psalms (CXIX:126), "It is time to work for God, for they have
made void Thy Torah," would apply. For the sake of Jewish
education the *melamdim* would be ready to comply with the
edict.

Halevy was on intimate terms with the foremost Russian
rabbinical personalities — relationships which remained constant
even after he left Russia for good. A day seldom went by without
some rabbinical visitors. In a rare personal note in his *Dorot
Harishonim*[18] Halevy mentioned that when the renowned R.
Naphtali Z. J. Berlin was visiting at his home he discussed with
him his views on the *Sheiltot*.[19] Halevy also recalled in one of

[18] Vol. III, p. 313.
[19] R. Berlin published a commentary on this Gaonic work.

his letters[20] that during the glorious days of the Volozhin Yeshiva he was instrumental in having R. Haim Soloveichik (R. Joseph Duber's son) appointed its *Rosh Mesivta* (head of the Yeshiva) and that R. Haim was his yearly house guest for months at a time.

R. Israel Salanter, after having met Halevy for the first time, wrote to R. Joseph Duber Soloveichik that he had made a rare find in Vilna.[21] Subsequently, whenever R. Israel stayed in Vilna he arranged many of his communal conferences in Halevy's home.

Halevy's close friendship with R. Haim Ozer Grodzensky of Vilna began when the latter was a young man.[22] From the time Halevy left Vilna in 1895, he entrusted to him his financial affairs[23] as well as the acquisition of a passport from Russia.[24] After Halevy settled in Germany in 1902 he corresponded with him as frequently as twice a week.[25] During this period R. Haim Ozer confided to Halevy that he was offered a rabbinical position in Wiesbaden by Baron Horace Guenzburg among others, and he was anxious to get his opinion as to whether he should accept it.[26]

R. Haim Ozer frequently solicited Halevy's advice regarding various communal matters.[27] R. Haim Ozer's role in the forefront of the Agudah movement which was launched by Halevy, was a natural outcome of their lifelong relationship. R. Haim Ozer also followed Halevy's historical writings with great interest.[28]

About six years after Halevy had left Russia, R. Haim Ozer wrote to him about the sorrowful state of affairs of Russian re-

---

[20] Halevy Number 103.

[21] S. Halevy, *op. cit.*, p. 19.

[22] Halevy was sixteen years older than Grodzensky.

[23] S. Halevy, *ibid.*, pp. 40-41.

[24] Halevy Numbers 44a, 83, 85, 96.

[25] B. S. Jacobson, *"Zikhronot,"* in *Sefer Zikaron Lerabbee Yitzhak Isaac Halevy,* p. 99.

[26] S. Halevy, *ibid.*, p. 44.

[27] See below pp. 37, 107.

[28] Halevy Number 26.

ligious Jewry.[29] He observed that a major factor in their dis-
organization was the lack of the type of leadership exemplified
by Halevy. One rabbinical personality, R. Yitzhak Ponevizer,
however, did not hesitate to remark, "What are we without R.
Eizik? Like orphans without a father."[30]

In 1891 a vigorous campaign was launched by the Russian
Society for the Prevention of Cruelty to Animals to outlaw
shehitah following the pattern of similar legislation in Germany.
Dr. Isaac Dembo,[31] the renowned physician of St. Petersburg, was
one of the most ardent and outstanding defenders of *shehitah*.
He took a leave of absence from his medical post for several
years to devote himself exclusively to this cause. A native of
Kovno, he was inspired in his youth by his contacts with R. Israel
Salanter and R. Joshua Leib Diskin. However, having been
deprived of a basic Jewish education, Dr. Dembo was anxious to
acquire a thorough understanding of the Jewish laws pertaining
to *shehitah*. At a conference in Kovno presided over by R. Isaac
Elchanan Spektor, Halevy was designated to provide him with the
fundamentals of *shehitah*. At first, Halevy corresponded with him
about this. Dr. Dembo, however, preferred to meet with Halevy
personally to review the entire subject and he spent eight days
at Halevy's home for this purpose.[32]

Few people were aware that it was Halevy who had prepared
the material for the much publicized address of Dr. Dembo at
the public conference with the Society for the Prevention of
Cruelty to Animals at the City Hall of Kovno on April 8, 1893,
which was attended by officials, noted physicians and veterinaries,
as well as R. Isaac Elchanan.[33] Ultimately the Government decided

---

[29] S. Halevy, *ibid.,* p. 43.
[30] *Der Israelit,* June 6, 1929, p. 2.
[31] *Jewish Encyclopedia,* VI, p. 512. His works on *shehitah* were translated into
several languages.
[32] S. Halevy, *ibid.,* pp. 21-23.

not to outlaw *shehitah* and it notified the Society to desist from its activities in this area. Contemporary records listed Halevy among the notables who attended the conference[33] and among the signatories of a letter sent by R. Isaac Elchanan to Dr. Dembo commending him for his invaluable services.[34] However, no mention was made of Halevy's work with Dr. Dembo behind the scenes.

Halevy was endowed with the gift of expression both in the written and in the spoken word. When the Hebrew weekly, *Halevanon*,[35] became the organ of Russian Orthodox Jewry in the beginning of the 1870's, Halevy anonymously contributed many forceful articles to its columns concentrating on subjects that were of vital concern to the religious community. With his penetrating observations and keen analytical mind he unmasked those who appeared with a religious facade, forcing them to reveal their true intentions. That Halevy's reputation in his early thirties was well established in the Jewish community at large is evidenced by a postscript to one of his articles by the publisher of the *Halevanon*[36] Jehiel Brill, who noted with regret that the author, "one of the renowned personalities in whom Torah, knowledge, faith and wisdom have well been combined," did not permit him to reveal his identity.

Halevy was particularly outspoken against the Reform movement that was under way in Russia. In the early 1870's the *Mefitzei Haskalah* (Society for the Propagation of Knowledge among the Jews) was negotiating with some Talmudic scholars in the Vilna area to edit a *"Shulhan Arukh* for modern times."[37] Their project was innocent enough — the publication of a Code

---

[33] *Hatzefirah,* 11 Iyar 5653, p. 343.
[34] J. Lipschitz, *Zikhron Yaakov,* III, pp. 211-213.
[35] Published in Mayence.
[36] Feb. 13, 1880, p. 229.
[37] S. Halevy, *op. cit.,* pp. 30-33; *Der Israelit,* May 30, 1929, p. 1.

of Jewish Law which would contain only the lenient decisions in areas of dispute between the two major authorities, R. Joseph Caro and R. Moshe Iserles, on each section of the *Shulhan Arukh*. Even some of the distinguished rabbis of Vilna did not realize at first the inherent dangers to Orthodoxy in this venture. In anonymous articles in *Halevanon* and *Hamelitz,* Halevy was among the first to point out the detrimental effects such a work would have upon Russian Jewry. In addition to his articles, Halevy's involvement led to their abandoning the entire project. Halevy's strategy was to go along with the proposition on the condition that the revised *Shulhan Arukh* would be edited in Vilna under the supervision of his rabbinical circle rather than in St. Petersburg which was the headquarters of the Society. As he had hoped, nothing further materialized.

Another intended project of this Society was the sponsorship of a rabbinical seminary for religiously uncommitted Russian students. Upon graduation they were expected to assume rabbinical posts in Russia as well as in the Holy Land. Halevy vigorously condemned these plans in the *Halevanon,*[38] in an article *"Divrei Shalom Vaemet,"*[39] pointing out that while it was plausible for the Society to popularize the study of the Russian language and other vital subjects among the rabbis through acceptable channels, the converse, to make rabbis of *maskilim* would be absurd. This article elicited a response from the famed scholar, Abraham Harkavy, who was an official of the Society, in *Halevanon.*[40] He attempted to justify the role of "modern" rabbis in appealing to nonconformists. Halevy, in turn, followed with two additional articles.[41] Again the *maskilim* retreated. In this series of articles

---

[38] Feb. 13, 1880, pp. 227-229.
[39] "Words of Peace and Truth" — a phrase from the Book of Esther IX:30.
[40] March 12, 1880, pp. 252-253.
[41] April 9, 1880, pp. 273-274; May 28, 1880, pp. 329-331.

symbols replaced Halevy's name: an inverted Hebrew *segol* in the former and several dots in quotes in the latter two.[42]

It should be noted that Halevy was not opposed to *haskalah* per se. Thus in his article rebutting Harkavy on the Seminary issue, Halevy lauded the work, *Zerubavel,* written by one of the founders of the *haskalah* movement, Isaac Ber Levinsohn, and he urged that it be translated into other languages. R. Isaac Elchanan of Kovno likewise "insisted that only rabbis with traditional training be recognized as religious leaders of the community... he took no exception to modern secular education in addition."[43]

Halevy was particularly disturbed by the fact that very few of the leading traditionally-minded personalities of stature in Russia were fluent in the vernacular and that secularists were drafted as a matter of necessity to represent the religious community in government circles.[44]

In his early days Halevy contributed scholarly articles in various periodicals, including the *Jeshurun,* edited by R. Samson Raphael Hirsch of Frankfurt.[45]

There is an interesting sidelight regarding an article in the journal, *Ben-Ami,*[46] edited by Jehuda Loeb Kantor, entitled, *"Kabalat Avot,"* by Yitzhak Isaac Halevy Rabinowitz. This work on the relationship between the Talmud *Bavli* and the Talmud *Yerushalmi* was incorporated in Halevy's first published volume of the *Dorot Harishonim*[47] in 1897. In a letter[48] addressed to Kantor dated 29 Iyar 5647 (May 23, 1887), Halevy requested the return of the article he had sent him for publication because

---

[42] This series of articles was reprinted by R. Jacob Lipschitz in a volume entitled, *Divrei Shalom Vaemet — Al Devar Sheaylah Hagedolah Sheaylat Harabbanut,* in 1884. Halevy's name was not mentioned here. However, in another work, *Zikhron Yaakov,* Volume III, p. 130, which was published posthumously in 1930, Lipschitz alluded to Halevy's authorship of these articles.

[43] I. Elbogen, *A Century of Jewish Life,* p. 222. [44] S. Halevy, *op. cit.,* p. 35.

[45] *Ibid.,* p. 51. [46] Issue of April-May 1887.

[47] Vol. III, pp. 111ff. [48] Halevy Number 1.

he did not deem it proper that his article appear alongside such writers as Moses Aaron Shatzkes (whose book, *Hamafteah,* created a stir in Orthodox circles on account of its radical views) and his disciple, Isaac Jacob Weissberg. He considered their works based on fantasies too abstruse to refute, in contrast with the writings of the German scholars who could be subjected to analytical criticism which would expose them. Halevy justified this rather bold step by referring to the Talmudic dictum[49] that it was the custom of the pious dignitaries of Jerusalem to refrain from attending a banquet unless they were aware of those who were invited with them. Halevy's letter was dated about the time this particular issue of the *Ben-Ami was* published.[50]

An article in letter form entitled, *"Mikhtav Lehair,"* under the name, Isaac Rabinowitz, appeared in Saul P. Rabinowitz's Hebrew translation of Graetz's *Divrei Yemei Yisrael, Volume* III edition of 1893.[51] It consisted of comments on S. P. Rabinowitz's earlier edition of the same volume, which Halevy asked him to insert in one of his later volumes.

It was Halevy's custom to make brief notations in the margins of the books he read. Unfortunately most of his library was lost in the course of his later wanderings.[52] Halevy's notes in his volume of Isaac H. Weiss's *Dor Dor Vedorshav* appear in Volume VI of the *Dorot Harishonim.*

Halevy's surname, Rabinowitz, was omitted from his signature in his correspondence as well as in his writings following his exodus from Russia in 1895.[53] On his tombstone, however, the family name, Rabinowitz, was inscribed.

---

[49] Sanhedrin 23a.   [50] It is possible that this letter was never dispatched.
[51] Pages 490-492.   [52] S. Halevy, *op. cit.,* p. 30.
[53] The only exceptions were his signatures with his surname, Rabinowitz, in two letters which he wrote in 1904, reprinted in M. H. E. Bloch's *Mee Nattan Limesheesah Yaakov Veyisrael Levozezim,* pp. 163-172. Inasmuch as the recipients of those letters, R. Moritz Guedemann and R. Joseph Bloch of Vienna, respectively, had known him by his Russian name Rabinowitz from his Vilna days, it was a practical matter to sign his full name when addressing them.

CHAPTER TWO

Between Vilna and Bad Homburg
(1895-1901)

I N THE PRIME OF HIS LIFE, both as a prominent rabbinical scholar and as a respected communal leader of financial means,[1] Halevy suddenly had to flee Russia in 1895 when his tea business failed as a result of an unsuccessful venture into a foreign tea exchange. This tragic event in his life was a blessing in disguise — for the publication of his monumental *Dorot Harishonim* and his masterful role as architect of the Agudath Israel movement came to fruition when he settled afterward in a new milieu.

His monetary obligations were still on his mind even after he left Russia. In his correspondence[2] from Germany Halevy referred to his past debts in Russia which distressed him and which he was endeavoring to repay. In another letter[3] he noted that the income of his newly published Volume Ic (in 1906) would help him towards covering his financial obligations in Russia. Halevy's son, Samuel,[4] recalled that his father kept careful records of his debtors whom he intended to compensate fully. On the other hand many who were indebted to him preferred the *status quo*.

On a page[5] among his papers, partly frayed and covered with

---

[1] In the *Hatzefirah* of 11 Iyar 5653, p. 343, reporting a conference in Kovno, there was a listing of rabbis, physicians, and men of means who were present. Halevy's name appeared among the latter.

[2] Fragment of a letter written after 1903.

[3] Halevy Number 17.

[4] *Op. cit.*, p. 38.

[5] Halevy Number 2. The text appears with parenthetical comments by his son Samuel, *ibid.*, pp. 36-37.

ink spots entitled, "This is my life," Halevy made notations of
his wanderings. He recorded his itinerary of a six year period on
thirty-three lines.[6] The first twenty-four lines were written in
Sadagura (Austria) under the date, 15 Tamuz 5657 (1897).

Halevy's exile began with "travail and fear" on Rosh Hodesh
Nisan 5655 (1895) until he managed to cross the border three
months later. During this period he passed through Hamlieh,
Noshkovka and Bobroysk, but his main stay was in Halmai.
Although faced with uncertainties and troubled by his son,
Mordecai Eliezer, he was still able to concentrate on his Talmudic
manuscripts that he had begun to write in his younger days. In
his commentaries which he entitled, *Battim Levaddim,* he analyzed
in depth basic Talmudic subjects, with special emphasis on the
many aspects of *sefaykot* (uncertainties).[7] Upon his arrival in

[6] Outline of Halevy's itinerary:

1 Nisan 5655	(1895)	Fled Vilna for Halmai via Hamlieh visited Noshkovka and Bobroysk
1 Tamuz 5655		Left for Pressburg via Kiev
4 Tamuz 5655		Arrived in Pressburg
1 Kislev 5656		Left Pressburg for London via Frankfurt
23 Kislev 5656		Left Frankfurt
24 Kislev 5656		Arrived in London
9 Sivan 5656	(1896)	Left London for Paris
1 Shevat 5657	(1897)	Left Paris for Pressburg — 10 day stay in Frankfurt en route from Pressburg to Vienna
11 Tamuz 5657		Left Vienna for Jassy, Rumania
12 Tamuz 5657		Arrived at Czernowitz, Austria, on the border of Rumania
13 Tamuz 5657		Detoured to nearby Sadagura
22 Tamuz 5657		Left Sadagura; went to Jassy
19 MarHeshvan 5658		Left Jassy
21 MarHeshvan 5658		Arrived in Frankfurt
17 Tevet 5658		Arrived in Bad Homburg
June 14	(1898)	Returned to Frankfurt
August		En route to Jassy via Sadagura
1 Elul 5658		Arrived in Jassy
8 MarHeshvan 5660	(1899)	Decided to return to Frankfurt
1 Adar 5661	(1901)	In Bad Homburg.

[7] *Der Israelit,* May 30, 1929, p. 2.

Pressburg (via Kiev, where he acquired his passport) on the fourth of Tamuz, he resumed his writing. After arranging for the publication of his *Battim Levaddim*,[8] he had to abandon the project for a more propitious time because of his financial limitations. Thus he turned to the final preparation of Volume III of his *Dorot Harishonim*: *The History and Literature of the Jews* which he felt would easily attract sponsors interested in his unique approach to *hokhmat Yisrael*. The five months that he spent in Pressburg were intellectually creative. Halevy took an active interest in the Yeshiva of Pressburg while he was there.

On Rosh Hodesh Kislev Halevy left for London via Frankfurt. He stayed in London for several months from the twenty-fourth of Kislev (December, 1895) until the ninth of Sivan, 1896, when he left for Paris.

During Halevy's initial visit in Frankfurt he had been befriended by R. Marcus Horovitz[9] of that city who welcomed him in his home and introduced him to the Chief Rabbi of Paris, R. Zadoc Kahn.

The latter, in turn, arranged for the French scholarly journal, *Revue d'Etudes Juives,* to publish a section of his manuscript of the *Dorot Harishonim* on the Saboraim (post-Talmudic sages) and the Gaonim who followed them, in a French translation.[10] Through this medium Halevy became known in scholarly circles in Western Europe. Kahn was also instrumental in having the *Alliance Israelite Universelle* of France sponsor the publication of his initial Volume III of the *Dorot Harishonim*. A page in this

---

[8] The first page of *Battim Levaddim* was reprinted in *Sefer Zikaron Lerabbee Yitzhak Isaac Halevy*, p. 38.

[9] Horovitz's efforts on his behalf are also noted by I. Heineman, "R. Mordecai Halevy Horovitz Utefeesat Hayahadut Shelo," *Sinai*, Tevet-Shevat 5704, p. 170.

[10] "La Cloture du Talmud et les Saboraim," 1896, pp. 1-17; 1897, pp. 241-250.

volume was dedicated by Halevy to Kahn in appreciation of his support.[11] Parenthetically, Kahn reneged on his written promise that the *Alliance* would publish Halevy's second volume. It was evident that his views were too extreme for Kahn's circles.[12]

After a nine months' stay in Paris, Halevy left for Pressburg on Rosh Hodesh Shevat, 1897, where he arranged for the printing of his book. As an expression of gratitude to Horovitz for his efforts as well as for his practical help, Halevy included in this volume[13] a letter from Horovitz commenting on this work.

That summer, on the night of the twenty-second of Tamuz, Halevy managed to cross the Austrian-Rumanian border from Sadagura, to join his daughter, Faiga, and son-in-law, Raphael Poker, in their home in Jassy, where he became a Rumanian citizen. It was there that he began to write Volume II of the *Dorot Harishonim.*

In the autumn of 1897 Halevy visited Frankfurt and on the seventeenth of Tevet he moved to the neighboring town of Bad Homburg where he remained until June 14, 1898. After another two months' stay in Frankfurt, he returned to Jassy on August 8, 1898. On the 8th of Heshvan, in the autumn of 1899, Halevy decided to leave Rumania for Frankfurt: "And so it was. I came straight to (Bad) Homburg and I printed my Volume II which was completed Rosh Hodesh Adar 5661 (1901)."

Volume II was dedicated by Halevy to Baron Wilhelm Carl de Rothschild,[14] the pious philanthropist, who had died a month

---

11 It was found only in the first edition.

12 S. Halevy, *op. cit.*, pp. 37-39. Halevy's appeal to Horovitz (Halevy Number 3a) to intervene again on his behalf did not bring about the hoped for results.

13 Pp. 307-310. The letter is dated 18 Sivan 5657.

14 J. Rosenheim in his *Zikhronot*, pp. 54-60, related personal biographical notes on the Baron.

before its completion. Among the Halevy papers was a draft[15] of a paean in honor of the Baron's seventieth birthday in 1898.

In the preface to Volume III which appeared in 1897, Halevy noted that he had originally intended to publish Volume II on the Talmudic era first, since he considered his studies on this subject primary for the understanding of the Mishnah and all other aspects of Torah. He delayed the completion of this volume because of his extended wanderings and the inaccessibility of books at that time. Yet he managed to publish Volume II before he settled in Germany.

The summer before the publication of Volume II of the *Dorot Harishonim,* Halevy had sent some of the sections of the book which had come off the press to R. Salomon Breuer of Frankfurt, the son-in-law and successor of R. Samson Raphael Hirsch. Halevy averred[16] that in this work he succeeded in restoring the sacred character of *hokhmat Yisrael* and of Jewish history.

[15] Halevy Number 2a.
[16] Halevy Number 5, dated Bad Homburg, 27 Tamuz 5660 (1900).

CHAPTER THREE

Klausrabbiner in Hamburg (1902-1914)

A SHORT TIME after Halevy's arrival in Germany he was invited to become the *Rabbiner* of the Leib Shaul *Klaus*[1] in Hamburg, one of a number of foundations established by those of means for subsidizing rabbinical scholars. In 1810 the founder of this *Klaus,* Leib *bar* Shaul, stipulated that its rabbis must be nonresidents of Hamburg and that they devote their time primarily to study.[2] They were not even to serve as *dayanim* (religious judges). This position was ideally suited for Halevy.

Among the Halevy letters is one dated Bad Homburg, 11 Tamuz 5660 (1900),[3] addressed to Hermann Gumpertz,[4] a Jewish communal leader in Hamburg, in which he indicated his readiness to accept the post of *Klausrabbiner.* It is evident from one of Halevy's letters to R. Marcus Horovitz of Frankfurt, written a month earlier,[5] that the latter also had a hand in this appointment. It was not until 1902, however, that Halevy took over the position.[6]

Inasmuch as Halevy's obligation as *Klausrabbiner* was only to give weekly lectures in Talmud, he took advantage of this

---

1 Eduard Duckesz, *Hakhmei AHU,* p. 111; Isaac Markon, "Isaac Halevy," *Encyclopedia Judaica,* VII, p. 867.

2 *Uebersicht aller wohlthaetigen Anstalten und Vereine so wie auch aller milden Stiftungen der deutsch and der portugiesisch israelitischen Gemeinde in Hamburg,* 1841, pp. 155-157.

3 Halevy Number 4.

4 He is listed in *Encyclopedia Judaica,* VII, p. 718.

5 Halevy Number 3, 3 Sivan 5660.

6 Minutes of the Executive Committee of the *Juedisch-Literarische Gesellschaft,* July 13, 1902.

grand opportunity to continue the writing of his *Dorot Harishonim* and to take a leading role in communal affairs.

The outstanding Talmudists of Hamburg attended Halevy's two-hour Talmudic expositions on Tractate *Hullin* on Saturday afternoons. Halevy had begun preparing for publication parts of his commentary on *Hullin* based on his lectures.[7]

In regard to his Talmudic studies Halevy observed[8] that if he were to find a *terutz* (answer) to a *kushya* (question), the *kushya* would still remain. He felt that is was essential to analyze the subject matter and trace the source of the problems in such a manner that the *kushya* would fall apart. The understanding of the subject should come either as a matter of course rather than being forced, or by a comparative analogy wherein another source may add further insight.[9]

Upon receiving a work by a renowned Galician Talmudist wherein eighty different explanations were applied to one major problem in the Talmudic Tractate *Zevahim,* Halevy observed, "The difference between the author of this work and myself is not great. That author searched for eighty solutions to one difficulty but I try to find one solution for eighty difficulties."

A number of *responsa* were found in the Halevy correspondence in answer to questions referred to him during his Hamburg days. The subjects included: the redemption of a first-born through an agent,[10] the disposition of a blemished first-born animal,[11] the redemption of a first-born child whose father was unknown,[12] permitting a wedding ceremony in the latter half of the Hebrew

---

[7] S. Halevy *op. cit.,* p. 50.
[8] *Der Israelit,* June 4, 1914, p. 3; May 30, 1929, p. 2.
[9] Based on *Talmud Yerushalmi Rosh Hashanah,* Chapter III, Halakhah 5.
[10] Halevy Number 75 to Kottek.
[11] Halevy Number 37 to Kottek.
[12] Halevy Number 145 to Kottek.

month,[13] and an interpretation of a *responsum* of *Rabbeinu Asher,* a classic Talmudic commentator.[14]

Two sets of correspondence between Halevy and R. Marcus Horovitz on Talmudic topics, appeared in the latter's *Matteh Levi.*[15]

Halevy, who was known in Hamburg as the Lithuanian Jew, initiated the custom of having his followers at his home on Simhat Torah and Purim, as was the custom in East European rabbinical circles. In his gentle voice, he would chant the traditional melodies which were popular in Vilna.[16] These gatherings were so well attended that his home could hardly accommodate all who came in ever increasing numbers from year to year.

Halevy was tall and of imposing stature, with a long full white beard. In Hamburg it was his custom to be attired at all times in a rabbinical frock coat and a top hat. He made an indelible impression upon the young and old alike with his dignified appearance and personality.

Halevy was a regular worshipper at the *Kehilat Yofee V'Agudat Yesharim* Synagogue in Hamburg.[17]

It was not long after Halevy settled in Germany that he resumed his active interest and influential role in Jewish communal life on the Continent as well as in the Holy Land. Thanks to the Halevy correspondence extant, a variety of events in which he was involved may now be brought to light.

The religious political scene in the Holy Land was of deep concern to Halevy. He was vehemently opposed to the pending

13 Halevy Number 155 to Kottek.
14 Halevy Number 46 to Grodzensky.
15 Part II, pp. 17-19, 64-66.
16 *Der Israelit,* June 4, 1914, p. 3.
17 In later years a silver plaque was affixed to his seat there in his memory.

controversial appointment in 1907 of R. Jacob Meir[18] as the Sephardic Chief Rabbi in Jerusalem. He had a hand in the preparation of an article on this subject in *Der Israelit*,[19] an Orthodox weekly published in Frankfurt. That Halevy kept abreast of events in the Holy Land was also indicated in his enthusiastic comments[20] when he had learned about the Pasha's friendly visit with the Hakham Bashi, the Sephardic Chief Rabbi, in 1908.

Halevy's intervention was sought in channeling a large sum of money in France to the Holy Land. He pursued this matter in his accustomed thoroughness.[21] Toward the end of 1908 Halevy was also involved in the appointment of the Chief Rabbi of Constantinople. Halevy had a hand in interesting the Rabbi of Cairo in this post,[22] while he agitated against the candidacy of R. Haim Nahoum.[23] He corresponded with some of the influential rabbis of Russia regarding this subject urging them to send their own letters of disapproval to the *Vaad Haruhani* (Religious Council) in Constantinople.[24]

It was in regard to this controversy that Halevy wrote to R. Haim Soloveichik,[25] delineating the role of the Turkish Chief Rabbinate. He pointed out that its occupant would not be merely a nominal authority such as the Russian *kozene rabbi* who was a government appointee to record marriages, etc., but would have complete jurisdiction over the local rabbis such as the power to hire and fire them. In a subsequent letter a month later he reminded R. Haim Ozer Grodzensky[26] that he had composed the

---

[18] He is listed in *Universal Jewish Encyclopedia*, VII, p. 445.
[19] Halevy Number 43.
[20] Halevy Number 81a.
[21] Halevy Numbers 28, 29.
[22] Halevy Number 84.
[23] He is listed in *Universal Jewish Encyclopedia*, VIII, p. 87.
[24] Halevy Number 85.
[25] Halevy Number 88a.
[26] Halevy Number 93.

text for a manifesto opposing the appointment of R. Nahoum, which was signed by both of them together with Rabbis Breuer and Hirsch (Frankfurt), Feilchenfeld (Posen), Adler (London), Ritter (Holland) as well as the Rabbis of Karlin and Brisk (Russia). Halevy noted with keen disappointment that even though the manifesto was published in the Jerusalem publications, *Hatzvi* and *Havatzelet*, R. Samuel Salant and a number of his colleagues in the Holy Land had sent greetings to R. Nahoum. History records nonetheless that R. Haim Nahoum Effendi became Chief Rabbi of Constantinople.

Another footnote to the history of Russian Jewry in the early 1900's has come to light through a letter to Halevy dated Vilna, 1905, from S. Fayvel Goetz,[27] an educator and an old acquaintance from their Vilna days. Goetz, having been apprised of the possible establishment of a seminary for Russian students in Frankfurt headed by R. Marcus Horovitz, appealed to Halevy to recommend him for the post of instructor of Russian language and history. Goetz was deeply disturbed by the inroads of the Bund[28] in Russian Jewish life and its imminent adverse effect on the religious education of his own children in particular — enough of a reason to leave Vilna.

Halevy's views on the contemporary Jewish scene found their way into his correspondence. Thus Halevy, scholarly by nature, was not impressed with the minimum standards of the newly ordained rabbis in Germany.[29] He suggested establishing a post-graduate seminary for them in Germany so that they could continue their studies for a number of years under a *gadol hador,* an outstanding rabbinical personality.[30]

The well-known Hildesheimer's Rabbinical Seminary in Berlin

---

27 Author of *Hadat Vehahinukh,* Vilna: Rom, 1896.
28 *Universal Jewish Encyclopedia,* IX, p. 585.
29 Halevy Number 86.
30 Halevy Number 142a.

was a target of Halevy's disfavor. He was critical of its permissiveness in publishing nontraditional views.[31] Religious inconsistencies in the policies of that Seminary were observed also by Jacob Rosenheim[32] during his stay in Berlin.

When in 1912 the *Vereinigung der liberalen Rabbiner Deutschlands* (Union of Liberal Rabbis of Germany) formulated their ideology in the *Richtlinien zu einem Program fuer das liberale Judentum* (Principles of a Program for Liberal Judaism), two hundred Orthodox rabbis signed a formal repudiation of this declaration. Halevy observed[34] that the text of the protest was "without life" and did not fully expose the motives of these Reform rabbis. He went so far as to compare the Reform movement with that of the early Christians who at first claimed that they were a Jewish group but in the course of time became anti-Jewish.

The degraded role of the Jewish religious communities in Russia was a problem that always vexed Halevy as well as the entire Russian rabbinate. In 1908 when Halevy learned that R. Haim Ozer Grodzensky was about to approach the Russian Government to reconsider its attitude toward the religious status of the Jews, he penned some salient points on this subject which he believed R. Haim Ozer would be able to utilize. In his rather lengthy letter to him Halevy noted[35] that the Government was gradually modifying the enforcement of its enlightenment movement that had been launched some sixty years before. However, there had not been any change in the Government's relation to the religious Jews although their spiritual leaders already had

---

[31] Halevy Number 59.

[32] *Zikhronot*, pp. 49-50.

[33] *Ibid.*, p. 104; N. Carlebach, *Joseph Carlebach and His Generation*, pp. 75-81; *Universal Jewish Encyclopedia*, IX, p. 469.

[34] Halevy Number 152a.

[35] Halevy Number 70.

manifested great interest in the development of general knowledge. Thus the enhancement of religion among the Jews would
bring in its wake a concommitant resurgence of education among
the youth in line with the aspirations of their elders. To concretize
their objective, Halevy suggested that it would be propitious for
the authorities to extend official recognition to the "religious"
rabbis who still had to take second place to their so-called enlightened brethren so that they could be instrumental in having
the young people who attended the *Gymnasium* excused from
writing on the Sabbath and Jewish festivals. He also urged that
Jews not be forbidden to work on Sunday. Their enforced idleness
on Sunday led many to work on Saturday for their livelihood; and
the desecration of the Sabbath, the cornerstone of the Jewish
religion, could result in the further weakening of the spiritual
fibre of the people. In this letter one beholds the master strategist,
Halevy, mapping out with ease practical approaches to weighty
problems.

The role of the *haskalah* within Jewish Orthodoxy was thought-
fully evaluated by Halevy. He took issue[36] with the Rabbi of
Pressburg who was of the opinion that the *haskalah* per se was
a spiritual danger to Russian Jewry. Halevy observed that because
students in the Russian *Gymnasium* were required to write on
the Sabbath, some Jewish families kept their children away. He
cited the *Torah im Derekh Eretz* philosophy of Samson Raphael
Hirsch, and its success in Germany where there were many
observant Jews who were physicians, chemists, and holders of
other prominent positions. Halevy realistically noted that the
world had already shrunk in his day and that the literature of
Germany, England and America managed to reach the Yeshiva
students in Russia through many channels, even if that were not
the case in Pressburg.

36 Halevy Number 159.

It is of interest to note that at the turn of the century Halevy was aware of the growing role of Jewish life and scholarship in the New World. Thus he planned to arrange for the distribution of his books in the United States.[37] When the Agudah movement was launched he saw the need to mobilize the religious forces in that country for the movement by sending an emissary there without delay.[38]

PUBLICATION OF DOROT HARISHONIM Ic, Ie, VI, and Id

Volume Ic of the *Dorot Harishonim*[1] was the first fruit of Halevy's pen in Hamburg. The *Juedisch-Literarische Gesellschaft* whose founding was spearheaded by Halevy,[2] sponsored the publication of this volume in 1906. Halevy's correspondence affords the reader intimate glimpses of his involvement with all aspects of the publication of this work, including its production, publicity, distribution, as well as the determination of its price and commission of its publisher.[3] His meticulousness encompassed the quality of the paper to be used for the book and the special type that he considered appropriate.[4] Since Halevy resided in Hamburg, he had difficulty in coordinating the schedule of the material and proofreading with the printer, Louis Golde, in Frankfurt.[5] The printer's lack of cooperation was a constant source of irritation to him.

The text of the title page Halevy saved for the last. He depended on his friend, Kottek, to help him with the German

---

[37] Halevy Numbers 28, 29.
[38] Halevy Number 160.

[1] From the last days of the Hasmonaim until the Roman procurators.
[2] See p. 44.
[3] Halevy Number 16.
[4] Halevy Number 10.
[5] Halevy Number 12.

text for the subtitle of the book.[6] Halevy's desire for perfection prompted him to make corrections in his works until the very last minute before going to press.[7]

When the completed volume reached Halevy in Hamburg he discovered a number of printer's errors. Halevy prepared a list of corrections in the German language, using Hebrew transliteration, and dispatched them to Kottek[8] at Bad Homburg with instructions to have them published in the weekly, Der Israelit, of nearby Frankfurt. It was evident that Halevy expected Kottek to submit to Der Israelit an edited German transcription of his text.[9] It is interesting to note that Halevy's first concern regarding his writings was for his immediate circle who were also subscribers to this Orthodox weekly.

Halevy anticipated a warmer reception for this volume than that given his previous books. He expected that gentile scholars would also purchase it.[10] He was pleased with the favorable reaction to the book[11] and took notice of the varied reviews.[12]

Halevy was ready to defend and elaborate upon his views. In response to the Jewish historian, Jawitz,[13] he clarified a number of questions relating to the volume. His reply to a critique by Leopold Landesberg in a draft which Halevy had ghostwritten for Kottek, was found, in part, among his correspondence.[14] Halevy also clarified a section of this volume for Kottek,[15] who was preparing an article in German.

---

[6] Halevy Number 23.
[7] Halevy Number 12.
[8] Halevy Number 26.
[9] These corrections, however, were not found anywhere in print.
[10] Halevy Number 17.
[11] Halevy Number 35.
[12] Halevy Number 29.
[13] Halevy Number 51.
[14] Halevy Number 42c. See p. 92.
[15] Halevy Number 78.

In Halevy's city, Hamburg, the headmasters of the Day Schools met at his home for the study of the *Dorot Harishonim*.[16]

The *Dorot Harishonim* was included in the list of textbooks of the Yeshiva of Lida (in the province of Vilna) upon the recommendation of S. Fayvel Goetz[17] who was appointed by the Russian Government in 1910 to review the Yeshiva's curriculum.[18] Halevy was particularly pleased with Goetz's gesture because it had always been his wish that his works would find their way into all Yeshivot. When the Rabbi of Lida, Isaac Jacob Reines, ordered the volumes for his Yeshiva from the *Juedisch-Literarische Gesellschaft,* Halevy sent Kottek a suggested text[19] for the Society's acknowledgment of his order noting that the author had agreed to one-half of the regular price. He concluded with the comment that the study of the *Dorot Harishonim* would prove helpful for the comprehension of the Mishnah and Talmud.

Two years before, in 1908, Halevy had arranged for a shipment of his books to a teacher in a "colony" in Petah Tikvah.[20] He could not resist stating that his writings would have a positive effect upon the spiritual outlook of the students there.

R. Abraham I. Kook wrote[21] to Halevy from the Holy Land that he was utilizing sections of the *Dorot Harishonim* in his lectures to his students and that he planned to give prominence to Halevy's writings in due time.

Halevy responded favorably to the request of R. Jacob Lipschitz of Kovno, and his son, Notel, in allowing a special rate for his volumes for the rabbis of Russia.[22] The text of an advertisement

---

[16] Halevy Numbers 41, 42.
[17] See above p. 36.
[18] Halevy Number 117.
[19] *Idem.*
[20] Halevy Number 62.
[21] A. I. Kook, *Igerot Hareiyah,* p. 308.
[22] Halevy Number 63.

by Notel in the Hebrew weekly, *Hamodia,*[23] was a composite
of Halevy's style extolling the unique role of the *Dorot Harishonim* in the interpretation of Jewish history.

In his introduction to Volume Ic, Halevy noted that he planned
to proceed with the era of the *Tannaim* in the projected Volume
Id. Following that section were to come Volumes Ia and Ib on
the early history of the Jews.

Six years after Volume Ic was published Halevy confided to
Kottek[24] that his material for the next volume was about ready
for publication. He estimated that the manuscript would total
about 1,400 pages. Since it was not practical to incorporate it
into one volume he had in mind to divide the text into two parts
and to print the second section, Volume Ie, first. Because of his
physical weakness he decided to have the manuscript ready beforehand instead of writing and proofreading simultaneously as he
had done previously.

The printing of Volume Ie of the *Dorot Harishonim,* also
sponsored by the *Gesellschaft,* was begun in 1913 with the
editorial assistance of Salomon Bamberger,[25] following the pattern
established for the previous volume. After seeing only one-fourth
of the text in print Halevy passed away on the twentieth of Iyar,
1914. Halevy's son, Samuel entrusted Bamberger with the completion of the volume which appeared in 1918. The manuscript
of Volume Id was entrusted by the Halevy family[26] resident in
Israel, to Moses Auerbach[27] who prepared it for publication in
1964.[28]

---

[23] Poltova, 23 Kislev 5672, p. 143.
[24] Halevy Number 142.
[25] Noted in his introduction to Volume Ie.
[26] Mrs. Samuel Halevy and her children.
[27] He settled in Israel as an educator under the aegis of Halevy.
[28] Published with *Sefer Zikaron Lerabbee Yitzhak Isaac Halevy.*

A section of the *Dorot Harishonim* on the era of the Bible was edited by Dr. Binyamin M. Lewin upon the request of Halevy's son, Samuel[29] in Jerusalem. Lewin recalled that in 1907 he had occasion to relate to Halevy that Nahum Sokolow had written an article acknowledging Halevy's stature in the field of the Oral Law but challenged his mastery of the Biblical era. Halevy reacted by interrupting his work on the Second Commonwealth for a time and delving into the field of Bible criticism. It was Lewin who was destined to publish part of this work in 1939, which he classified as Volume VI.

Unfortunately other Halevy manuscripts in Lewin's possession were lost.[30]

[29] Introduction to Volume VI of the *Dorot Harishonim*.
[30] Related by a member of the Halevy family.

CHAPTER FOUR

Mentor of the
Juedisch-Literarische Gesellschaft

WHEN ISAAC HALEVY at the age of 52 arrived in Germany, his reputation as a unique Torah personality and author of the *Dorot Harishonim* attracted a following of young rabbinical scholars. The negative reception given Halevy by the circle of historians whom Halevy criticized in his works must have brought Halevy to the realization that in order to cultivate his school of thought a scholarly milieu for the promulgation of the Orthodox interpretation of Jewish history would have to be created. He lost no time in becoming the inspiring force of the young rabbis which in turn led to the founding of the *Juedisch-Literarische Gesellschaft* (Jewish Literary Society) in 1901 with Frankfurt as its headquarters.[1] Joining Halevy in the Society were Salomon Bamberger, Eduard Biberfeld, Jonas Bondi, Heimann Kottek and Gerson Lange, all prominent leaders in Orthodox communities.

Halevy alluded[2] to the *Gesellschaft's* coming into being in the wake of the *Dorot Harishonim* and noted[3] that its *raison d'etre* was to further his "new approach" in Jewish scholarship. He also viewed the Society as a vital link between the Orthodox community and an Orthodox orientated scholarship.[4]

One of the early actions of the members of the *Gesellschaft*

---

[1] Isaac Markon, *"Juedisch-Literarische Gesellschaft," Encyclopedia Judaica,* IX, p. 558.

[2] Halevy Number 42b.

[3] Halevy Number 38.

[4] Halevy Number 18.

was to grant Halevy an annual stipend at the time of his appointment as *Klausrabbiner* in Hamburg so that he would be able to continue his research undisturbed.[5] Halevy referred[6] to the allocations from the *Gesellschaft* several years later in his correspondence.

It was also due to Halevy's initiative that the *Jahrbuch*, the annual journal of the *Juedisch-Literarische Gesellschaft*, was launched. It appeared regularly beginning with 1903 and semi-annually from 1912 until 1932.

The role of the *Jahrbuch* in bringing to light Halevy's approach to Jewish scholarship was no secret.[7] Many articles by Halevy's followers were in consonance with their master's views, especially those of Bondi, Kottek, Isak Unna and Halevy's son, Samuel.[8]

The adoration among the members of the *Gesellschaft* for Halevy remained throughout their lives. Gerson Lange, director of the *Realschule der Israelitischen Religions Gesellschaft* of Frankfurt, became Halevy's ardent admirer from the time they first met.[9] He headed the *Juedisch-Literarische Gesellschaft* from its beginning until his death in 1923. Salomon Bamberger of Hanau was entrusted by Halevy with the editing of Volumes Ic and Ie of the *Dorot Harishonim*. His reverence for Halevy was eloquently expressed in his introduction to Volume Ie which was published after Halevy's death. Bamberger was also editor of the *Jahrbuch* published by the Society. Jonas Bondi of Mainz

---

[5] Minutes of Executive Committee of the *Juedisch-Literarische Gesellschaft*, July 13, 1902.

[6] Halevy Number 83 (in 1909).

[7] K., "*Das III. Jahrbuch der Juedisch-Literarischen Gesellschaft*," *Der Israelit*, July 20, 1906, pp. 9-10.

[8] See "*Verzeichnis der Autoren und ihrer Arbeiten*," in the *Jahrbuch*, Vol. XX (1929), Appendix, pp. 23ff.

[9] J. Rosenheim, *Zikhronot*, p. 77.

was reputed to have studied by heart almost every line of the
Dorot Harishonim.[10]

Heimann Kottek's close friendship with Halevy began in
1898 when the latter first visited the resort town of Bad Homburg
near Frankfurt, where Kottek was rabbi. Kottek was on the
executive committee of the *Gesellschaft* as well as on the editorial
board of the *Jahrbuch*. Kottek's key role in the *Gesellschaft* was
evidenced in the volume, *Admat Kodesh,* a geography of the
Holy Land, which the author, Isaac Goldhor, dedicated to Kottek
in appreciation of his efforts in making possible its publication
by the Society. (Halevy had previously written to Kottek[11] that
this work was worthy of the Society's sponsorship even though
he disagreed with some of the author's points.)

In the collection of over one hundred and twenty-five Halevy
letters to Kottek more than half were concerned in large measure
with all aspects of the affairs of the *Gesellschaft* and its publications. The correspondence relating to the *Gesellschaft* reflected
Halevy's ideas and his approach to Jewish scholarship.

That Halevy was the guiding spirit of the *Gesellschaft* and that
he played a decisive role in its development were also revealed
in the Halevy correspondence. Halevy's views were seriously
sought by the *Gesellschaft* in regard to sponsoring literary
works as well as in accepting articles for publication in its
Jahrbuch. After several years' publication Halevy was gratified
to observe[12] that the *Jahrbuch* had made its mark in Jewish
scholarship. A number of years thereafter he again had occasion to
express his satisfaction with its progress.[13]

Halevy edited some of the articles which appeared in the

---

10 B. S. Jacobson, *Zikhronot,* p. 79.
11 Halevy Number 138.
12 Halevy Number 47 (5667).
13 Halevy Number 113 (5670).

Jahrbuch.[14] Halevy also suggested[15] revisions to Bamberger, the editor, who visited him weekly regarding the *Jahrbuch.*[16] One of Halevy's titles within the *Gesellschaft* could have been "Editor's Editor."

Not all the articles, however, were seen by Halevy before publication. (Halevy's residence in Hamburg was a day's travel to Frankfurt.) Halevy was particularly disturbed[17] by an article already published wherein he detected some misinterpretations of Judaism. Nor did Halevy hesitate to criticize the works of his own followers.[18] Such matters as meeting deadlines also concerned Halevy. He insisted that the publication of the *Jahrbuch* not be held up even if it meant omitting an article from that issue.

Among the Halevy papers were two drafts of a letter to Isak Unna[20] acknowledging his request for material relating to an article he was in the midst of preparing for the *Jahrbuch.* Halevy could not resist concluding his remarks with a plea for more literary contributions from the Orthodox circles.

While Halevy differed with some individuals, it did not necessarily follow that they would be alienated from the *Gesellschaft.* In a letter to his son, Samuel,[21] Halevy expressed deep concern about the many young scholars who drifted into the "enemy camp," such as the straying of Siegmund Jampel. Halevy was anxious to attract scholars to the *Jahrbuch* in order to wean them away from negative religious influences. He urged Kottek[22] to

14 Halevy Numbers 27, 37, 53.
15 Halevy Number 43.
16 Halevy Number 120.
17 Halevy Number 79.
18 Halevy Number 107.
19 Halevy Numbers 20, 47.
20 Halevy Numbers 7, 7a, 7b.
21 Halevy Number 76.
22 Halevy Numbers 28, 37.

encourage Salomon Funk to contribute material to the *Jahrbuch* as long as it was worthwhile even though he was aware of the fact that Funk did not subscribe to his views.

While there were no signed articles by Halevy in the *Jahrbuch*, the Halevy correspondence[23] revealed that he had written a comprehensive "Editor's Reply,"[24] which was translated from his Hebrew into German, in response to an article by R. David Hoffmann on the subject of the Sanhedrin.[25]

Halevy was a very active ghostwriter for the administration of the *Gesellschaft*. He often sent Kottek drafts of letters which were to be written in German in the name of the *Gesellschaft*.[26] One such text,[27] meant for Jehiel Michael Pines[28] who lived in the Holy Land, concerned the solicitation of material for the *Jahrbuch*. Halevy noted that the scope of the yearbook embraced all branches of *hokhmat Yisrael* and Jewish history. He suggested that Pines prepare an article relating to the history of the cities in the Holy Land or on "antiquities." Arrangements for having the article translated into German and financial details were mentioned.

Another draft,[29] this one from Halevy directly to R. Jacob Lipschitz of Kovno who was the private secretary of R. Isaac Elchanan Spektor for many years, referred to a request for the manuscript of the late Eliezer Atlas relating to the "Council of the Four Lands." This work however never saw the light.

It was also Halevy's suggestion[30] that Moses Auerbach[31] was

---

[23] Halevy Number 60.
[24] *"Nachbemerkung der Redaktion,"* V (1907), pp. 238-244.
[25] See below p. 81.
[26] Halevy Numbers 26, 42.
[27] Halevy Number 27a.
[28] He is listed in *Universal Jewish Encyclopedia,* VIII, p. 535.
[29] Halevy Number 23a.
[30] Halevy Number 82.
[31] Author of *Toledot Am Yisrael.*

to have been formally informed by the *Gesellschaft* that it would be pleased to sponsor his brochure when it would be ready for publication. On the other hand, Halevy[32] vetoed the request of R. Hirsch Hildesheimer that the *Gesellschaft* underwrite a work on the Jews of Russia by Saul P. Rabinowitz, the Hebrew translator of Graetz's history. Halevy averred that Rabinowitz, whom he had known personally during his Vilna days, would not treat the rabbinical personalities with the proper reverence while he would go out of his way to praise the efforts of the *maskilim.*

Though Halevy was severely critical of the writings of Leopold Landesberg[33] he urged[34] that his works be sponsored by the *Gesellschaft* providing the material would be reviewed beforehand. He believed that in this manner some positive influence would be exerted upon the author. When some galleys of Landesberg's work reached Halevy,[35] however, he realized that his hopes had not materialized. Since the *Gesellschaft* had decided to send Landesberg a sum of money Halevy suggested that Landesberg be informed that the *Gesellschaft* could not sponsor his work, but it would send him 150 marks when it would be published.

Halevy's wishes however, were not always fulfilled. Michael Jacobson had prepared a defense of Halevy's views for inclusion in the same issue of the *Jahrbuch* of 1906 which was to have had an article containing a critical reference to Halevy by Salomon Funk.[36] When Bamberger rejected it, Halevy gave vent to his feelings of disappointment in a letter to Kottek.[37] Nonetheless, Jacobson's article did not see print.

---

[32] Halevy Number 115.
[33] Author of *Hikrei Lev.* He is listed in the *Encyclopedia Judaica,* X, p. 612.
[34] Halevy Number 62.
[35] Halevy Number 73.
[36] Halevy Number 37.
[37] Halevy Number 38.

Another activity of the *Gesellschaft* was the sponsorship of public lectures.[38] Halevy was very disturbed when he learned[39] that a lecture on "Philo and the *Halakhah*" was to be given by one who, in his opinion, would base his talk on references that were not in accord with tradition. Realizing that the chances of changing the program were nil, he urged Kottek to prepare himself for this occasion. He suggested that Kottek review the Philo material in the *Meor Einayim* (which attributed Philo's major source of Jewish knowledge to the non-Hebrew *Septuaginta*) and to his own references in the *Dorot Harishonim*.[40] He even gave Kottek detailed instructions in locating the *Meor Einayim* in the Frankfurt Library.

The range of Halevy's concern for the *Gesellschaft* also encompassed its financial interests and its prestige. Thus, having heard of a legacy that R. Marcus Horovitz of Frankfurt was to distribute to charity, he hastened to urge Kottek[41] to contact him on behalf of the *Gesellschaft*. He likewise suggested[42] that the *Gesellschaft* invite Horovitz and his son, Jacob, to join the writers' roster of the *Jahrbuch,* thereby gaining the friendship of their influential circle, which was apart from the Hirsch-Breuer community of Frankfurt.

Halevy was most outspoken, however, when he received word[43] that Ahron Marcus[44] was to be appointed executive secretary of the *Juedisch-Literarische Gesellschaft.* He was convinced that this plan would not serve the best interests of the *Gesellschaft* and that it would be better for the *Gesellschaft* to disband rather

---

[38] Halevy Number 102.
[39] Halevy Number 116.
[40] Vol. Ic, pp. 127, 129.
[41] Halevy Number 11.
[42] Halevy Number 46.
[43] Halevy Number 37a.
[44] He is listed in the *Universal Jewish Encyclopedia,* VII, p. 348.

than compromise its idealism by engaging as its spokesman one unworthy of the trust.

The *Jahrbuch* had a section for unpublished classical manuscripts. Halevy was interested in the acquisition of some of the manuscripts from the Elkan Adler[45] collection in London for the *Jahrbuch*.[46] He thought that such material would enhance the prestige of the *Gesellschaft*. Since there was some hesitancy on the part of Adler to publish the manuscripts, Halevy suggested that he be assured that they would be known as the Adler Collection.

Halevy was in favor[47] of having the *Gesellschaft* cooperate with the *Mekize Nirdamim*,[48] a society devoted to the publication of old manuscripts and books. He pointed out to Kottek the long range of advantages of this venture and he suggested some strategy for overcoming the possible objections of a number of their colleagues.

The *Juedisch-Literarische Gesellschaft* also sponsored the publication of Volume Ie of the *Dorot Harishonim* in 1919—a fitting tribute to its guiding spirit.

---

[45] He is listed in *op. cit.*, I, p. 90.

[46] Halevy Number 53.

[47] Halevy Number 40.

[48] *Universal Jewish Encyclopedia*, VII, p. 449.

CHAPTER FIVE

His Role in Historiography

IT WAS RATHER UNUSUAL for a leading personality in Russian rabbinical circles who was also an official of the famed Volozhin Yeshiva to be drawn concurrently into *hokhmat Yisrael*. As early as 1887, while in his prime in Vilna, Halevy disclosed in a letter to Dr. Jehuda Loeb Kantor,[1] editor of the journal, *Ben-Ami,* his reason for delving into the prevalent Jewish scholarship. He noted that he was not involving himself in *hokhmat Yisrael* for self aggrandizement, but only because he was appalled by the deep inroads into Jewish life made by the Russian *maskilim* who, following in the footsteps of the German scholars, falsified Jewish history and made every effort to ensnare the youth. He felt impelled to unmask them and to reveal their deception.

While Halevy in his day must have had sufficient reasons for his accusations, it is of poignant interest that a biographer[2] of Leopold Zunz, the founder of the "Science of Judaism," candidly recorded that Zunz's "hostility towards the Talmud was quite outspoken. He believed that 'as long as the Talmud is not dethroned, nothing can be done' . . . Zunz considered taking the road of many young gifted Jews of the period: baptism."

The defense of tradition in Jewish scholarship became Halevy's holy mission. In the midst of the publication of his second

---

[1] Halevy Number 1.

[2] Nahum N. Glatzer, *Leopold and Adelheid Zunz — An Account in Letters* 1958, pp. XV-XVI.

volume of the *Dorot Harishonim* in 1900 he wrote to R. Salomon Breuer[3] of Frankfurt that he considered his work a step in the restoration of the sanctity of Jewish history. Halevy pursued this goal with unmitigated zeal in all his writings.

The savant, R. David Hoffmann,[4] observed that Halevy was the one who succeeded in refuting the heretofore unchallenged hypotheses of the *maskilim* who were inimical to Jewish tradition. Halevy was primarily up in arms against their motivations which he felt duty-bound to repudiate.

Halevy was deeply perturbed that his contemporary *hokhmat Yisrael* was not sensitive to the unique spiritual heritage of the Jews.[5] He compiled ample evidence that the popular Jewish scholars parroted the Bible critics on the role of the prophets,[5a] calumniated our Sages[6] and espoused reform Judaism.[7]

In one *j'accuse*[8] Halevy pointed out how the historians attempted to minimize the role of the Jewish people in the Second Commonwealth and thus do away with the fundamental concepts of tradition. He likewise accused them of being slaves to their subjective notions[9] such as the postdating of the Torah and the Oral Law. It was precisely in those areas where they slandered Jewish tradition that he felt the need to restore the breach.[10] Thus in his writings he delved especially into those chapters of Jewish history which were not treated in consonance

[3] Halevy Number 5.
[4] From a tribute in *Sefer Zikaron Lerabbee Yitzhak Isaac Halevy*, p. 109.
[5] *Dorot Harishonim* Ie, p. 317.
[5a] *Ibid.*, p. 109.
[6] *Ibid.*, p. 373; Ic, p. 484.
[7] *Ibid.*, Ie, p. 392.
[8] *Ibid.*, Ic, pp. 113-114.
[9] *Ibid.*, footnote, p. 360.
[10] *Ibid.*, Ie, 373.

with Jewish tradition. He did not hesitate to lock swords with scholars from all schools.

The historian Wolf Jawitz,[11] in his exposition of Halevy's historical method, observed that scholars like Graetz did not approach the study of Jewish history with reverence for the sacred elements of tradition. Where any historical source differed from the accepted traditional viewpoint, there was no question where the loyalty of these Jewish scholars lay—they were more concerned with fitting Jewish historical events and values into the framework of higher criticism and other prevalent philosophies of history than in reconstructing the history of the Jews in terms of their inner spiritual core.

Mordecai (Markus) Elias[12] likewise pointed out that the nineteenth century Jewish historians, influenced by the schools of neo-humanism and Bible criticism, based their writings on the philosophy of enlightenment and natural evolution. As valid as this approach might have been in interpreting the spiritual history of other nations, Halevy forcefully fought this viewpoint in relation to the Jews. Halevy saw in the crystallization of the Oral Law a unique historical process that suggested a special perspective for its interpretation. It is in this light that Elias discerned Halevy's preoccupation with the subject matter of Volume III of the *Dorot Harishonim* which he wrote first. In contrast with the prevalent views of Jewish historians who looked upon the Talmudic and Gaonic periods as an era of spiritual stagnation, Halevy stressed the vital role of the *Amoraim,* the sages of the Talmudic era, and the *Gaonim,* who followed them, in the preservation and transmission of historic Judaism. It was this positing of the *elan vital* of the unbroken chain of Jewish

[11] Introductory essay in Vol. VI of his *Toledot Yisrael.*
[12] "R. Yitzhak Isaac Halevy," *Ishim Udemuyot Behokhmat Yisrael,* edited by S. K. Mirsky, pp. 67-75.

tradition from the Prophets to the *Gaonim* that prompted Halevy to begin his writings of Jewish history in reverse chronological order with the literature of the last representatives of the Talmudic era, the Gaonim.[13]

Among the noted historians who were the main subjects of Halevy's polemics were Zacharias Frankel, Abraham Geiger, Heinrich Graetz, Nachman Krochmal, and Isaac H. Weiss, as well as the non-Jewish scholars Abraham Kuenen, Theodor Mommsen, Emil Schuerer, and Julius Wellhausen. Thus when Halevy began to write on the Biblical era he noted[14] that he was continuing his policy of refuting the outstanding spokesmen of that literature just as he had done in his previous works.

It should not be inferred that everything which was written by the "German scholars" was objectionable to Halevy. In the *Dorot Harishonim* he unhesitatingly referred the reader to Graetz or Schuerer in the course of some subject that he was expounding.

Nor was his research limited. Besides the many scholars mentioned in his works, he read such contemporaries as Hermann L. Strack and Judaica journals as *Hagoren*.

In the annals of Jewish history, Halevy was not the first to take up the cudgel in defense of an uncompromising traditional viewpoint. Samson Raphael Hirsch (1808-1888) was known for his polemics against Frankel and Graetz among others.[15] Another work defending the sanctity of the Oral Law was published in Frankfurt in 1861 by Tzvi Binyamin Auerbach entitled *Hatzofeh Al Darkei Hamishnah.*

---

[13] See also S. Halevy, *"Avee Zikhrono Livrakhah," Sefer Zikaron Lerabbee Yitzhak Isaac Halevy,* pp. 51-52.

[14] Vol. VI, p. 3.

[15] Joseph Elias, *Reason, Revelation, and History in 19th Century Jewish Thought.* Thesis, University of Chicago, 1946.

M. Y. Gleicher, *"Rabbi Yitzhak Isaac Halevy," Kol Yisrael,* Jerusalem, 15 Iyar 5706, p. 2.

A posthumous work, the *Dor Yesharim,* by R. Yehuda Lip-schitz, published in Russia in two parts (1907 and 1910), was concerned solely with refuting I. H. Weiss's *Dor Dor Vedorshav* on the Biblical era and the Oral Law. Lipschitz pointed out that Weiss followed in the footsteps of the Bible critic Franz Delitzsch, and he discounted the authenticity of the Mosaic Law as well as the Oral Law. Quoting substantial excerpts from the *Dor Dor Vedorshav,* Lipschitz cited instance after instance of consistently flagrant misinterpretations of the Biblical and Talmudic texts. Lipschitz referred to Halevy's views in his work.[16]

Mention should also be made of the literary accomplishments of such renowned scholars within the pale of Orthodoxy as R. Haim Heller, R. David Hoffmann and Wolf Jawitz. It is Halevy, however, who has been considered the foremost spokesman of the traditional school of Jewish history.[17] Halevy's efforts in this field did not go unappreciated by the rabbinate of his day.[18]

Halevy's methodology in Jewish history was delineated in his letter to R. Abraham I. Kook[19] as being a serious attempt to understand the source materials objectively, rather, than as a "new approach" per se. He felt that even the *Rishonim,* the early commentators on the Talmud, such as Rashi and Maimonides, would have been pleased with his historical studies of the Mishnah and Talmud. The fundamental principle which guided him in his historical studies, he noted, was to find the master

16 Part I, pp. 11, 91.

17 J. L. Fishman (Maimon) in his introductory essay to Volume VI of the *Dorot Harishonim* understood Halevy's role as defender of tradition. S. K. Mirsky in the introductory essay in *Ishim Udemuyot Behokhmat Yisrael* pp. 5-64, also designated Halevy first place.

18 R. Haim Ozer Grodzensky's tribute (among others) in the introduction of Yehuda Lipschitz's *Dor Yesharim;* and R. Aaron Walkin's in Jacob Lipschitz's introduction in *Zikhron Yaakov,* Vol. I, p. 13.

19 Halevy Number 80.

key which could solve a number of questions pertaining to some subject as a whole, rather than interpret each point singly. Halevy expressed a similar viewpoint in regard to the proper understanding of the Talmud.[20]

By his method of objective questioning Halevy was able to discern the essence of the facts that might have been camouflaged many times over.[21] Halevy would therefore trace the conclusions of others by going back to the primary sources of the subject matter and evaluating them accordingly. Thus he incorporated the sources in his writings so that his readers could follow the manner in which he reached his conclusions.

In the study of the Oral Law, Halevy stressed the necessity of applying the inductive method of careful analysis of the source materials in contrast to the deductive (inferential) method prevalent among historians.[22]

Halevy's forte was his mastery of Jewish sources coupled with his own penetrating analysis of other primary sources to the extent that the historical kernels could be expertly shelled in the process of interpretation without distorting their original form.

It was in the antiquities of Jewish tradition that Halevy beheld the foundations of the eternal glory of Judaism. To him Jewish tradition had a sound basis within the arena of world history. Halevy was convinced that the Roman sources and the Jewish sources could be reconciled.[23] Thus he went to great lengths to harmonize the Talmudic sources with Josephus as

[20] See above p. 33.
[21] J. B. M., *"Halevy's wissenschaftliche Methode."* Der Israelit, April 29, 1915, p. 3; May 6, 1915, p. 2.
[22] Ph. Frankl, *"Das neue Jahrbuch der Juedisch-Literarischen Gesellschaft."* Der *Israelit,* Aug. 15, 1907, pp. 11-12.
[23] *Dorot Harishonim* Ie, pp. 589, 593ff.

well as with the Greek and Roman sources. Nor were numisma-
tology[24] and the Christian Bible[25] outside his province.

Halevy's mastery of the Talmud was interwoven into the
pattern of his studies in contrast with the many historical works
on that period whose authors did not possess the intrinsic
knowledge and grasp of this phenomenal literature.

Halevy made emendations of Talmudic texts whenever he
detected copyists' errors.[26] He referred to this problem in a
letter to his son[27] in connection with the manuscripts of the
Igeret Rav Sherira Gaon. Halevy likewise did not hesitate to
take issue with the historical views of the post-Talmudic commentators, notwithstanding his reverence for them, where his
studies of the Talmudic sources were not in consonance with
theirs.[28]

Halevy emphasized in his writings that he was concerned
with presenting an objective picture of Jewish history from a
scholarly point of view rather than a religious viewpoint.[29]
Thus he noted[30] that he was attempting to avoid such proof that
was subject to question.

Of interest in this regard is the observation of the historian
Solomon Judah Loeb Rapoport (died 1867), whose writings in
hokhmat Yisrael preceded Halevy's: "I have already told you
that as I sit down to investigate matters of this kind (involving
application of critical investigation of problems pertaining to
religious law) I free myself from bias and from all emotional
feelings flowing out of religious zeal, for I know indeed that

---

24 *Ibid.,* Ic, pp. 64, 228, 399, 613, 617; Ie, pp. 350, 591, 602, 633.
25 *Ibid.,* Ic, p. 630.
26 *Ibid.,* p. 470; Ie, p. 619.
27 Halevy Number 76.
28 M. Elias, *op. cit.,* p. 113.
29 *Dorot Harishonim* Ic, Introduction and p. 429; Ie, p. 40.
30 *Ibid.,* p. 592.

every objective and unbiased investigation results in a more intensive strengthening of our holy Torah and our true religion."[31]

In soliciting an article from Yehiel M. Pines[32] for the *Jahrbuch* of the *Juedisch-Literarische Gesellschaft* (the text of the letter was written by Halevy), he stressed the importance of scholarly standards. He likewise urged the editors of the *Gesellschaft* to accept articles for the *Jahrbuch* and for publications of popular interest which were based on scholarly proofs rather than on conjecture.[33]

When he learned that plans were under way to "popularize" the *Jahrbuch,* he vetoed the idea by pointing out that the reputation of Orthodoxy in scholarly circles, thanks to the scholarly attainments of the *Jahrbuch,* would be lost thereby.[34] Thus Halevy derided one author who neglected to utilize the Greek sources in his work.[35]

In the founding phases of the Agudath Israel movement of which he was the foremost architect, Halevy emphasized that the foundations of Orthodoxy were based upon true *hokhmat Yisrael.*[36] He stressed also the significance of undiluted scholarship in the Agudah's publications.[37]

To Halevy the keys to understanding the Biblical and post-Biblical eras were the *halakhic* (law) sources in the Mishnah and Talmud, in contrast with the limited role of the *aggadah* (lore), which was contingent upon subjective interpretations.[38]

---

[31] S. Pitlik, "S. L. Rapoport's Historical Method." *Jewish Quarterly Review,* XXXI (October, 1940), p. 125.

[32] Halevy Numer 27a.

[38] Halevy Numbers 17, 42a, 42b, 80; *Dor. Har.,* Ic, p. 477; Ie, p. 77;

[34] Halevy Number 90.

[35] Halevy Number 119.

[36] Halevy Number 134.

[37] Halevy Number 110.

[38] Halevy Numbers 17, 42a, 42b, 80; *Dor. Har.,* Ic, p. 477; Ie, p. 77; *Entziklopedia Talmudit,* Vol. I, p. 62.

Thus the *aggadah* could serve as a bolster to conclusions based on the *halakhah*.[39] On the other hand, R. Abraham I. Kook,[40] in his correspondence with Halevy, came to the defense of the *aggadah* and stressed the dual roots of *halakhah* and *aggadah* in Jewish life.[41]

It was in a letter to Kook[42] in 1908 that Halevy pointed out that the study of Jewish history, as in the *Dorot Harishonim*, would be a leading factor in bringing about a needed spiritual resuscitation in the Holy Land at the time. Halevy was convinced that the mastery of Jewish history would provide further illumination of the Torah as well as the resources with which to combat the "enemies of the Almighty." He cited Kook's historical writings as a case in point.

In his correspondence Halevy attempted to clarify the unusual order and structure of the subject matter in his *Dorot Harishonim*. In answer to an author[43] who asked him for his references on a particular topic, Halevy noted that his work was not written according to the chronology of personalities. It was meant rather to be a history of the Jewish people and of the main streams wherein the personalities and the events flowed. In acknowledging Jawitz's[44] query relating to the omission of some major subjects in the *Dorot Harishonim* Halevy noted that he never had in mind to write an ordinary history of the Mishnah and Talmud, or to repeat the events recorded in Josephus as well as other well known facts. His aim was to recreate the history of the Jewish people of which the Mishnah and Talmud were integral elements; to shed light on the major

---

[39] M. Elias, *op. cit.*, p. 113.
[40] *Igerot Hareiyah*, Nos. 103 and 146.
[41] S. K. Mirsky, *op. cit.*, pp. 35-37.
[42] Halevy Number 80.
[43] Isak Unna, Halevy Number 7b.
[44] Halevy Number 47a.

events of the glorious, multi-faceted panorama of the Jewish people; and to rediscover the spiritual forces in the lives of our sages of yore.

In the *Dorot Harishonim* Halevy called attention to his clarification of the Talmudic view of Jewish history[45] and to the conceptual approach in his historical studies.[46]

Halevy's writing of history was centered around the works of others rather than his own planned structure. His *Dorot Harishonim* consisted primarily of critical studies and polemics on varied subjects as well as reinterpretations of the related material under discussion. It may be that his philosophy of purpose had affected him to the point that he could write in no other manner.

Halevy, nonetheless, felt the need for a revision of his works which would follow some historical order. It was the realization of this shortcoming in his books that prompted him to call upon others to prepare historical works based on his writings with his guidance and help. The *Juedisch-Literarische Gesellschaft* was also committed to sponsor their publication. Halevy prepared a draft of a letter that was sent by the *Gesellschaft* to Leopold Landesberg,[47] author of the historical work *Hikrei Lev,* in which it was suggested that he devote several years writing a history based on the *Dorot Harishonim* with the support of the *Gesellschaft.*

Halevy was interested in having Jawitz rewrite his history *Toledot Yisrael,* according to the *Dorot Harishonim,* with the sponsorship of the *Gesellschaft.* This project, however, did not get under way because there was no meeting of minds.[48] A

---

[45] Volume Ie, p. 247.
[46] *Ibid.,* pp. 372-373.
[47] Halevy Number 42a. See below page 92.
[48] See also page 83.

draft of a Halevy letter[49] to another scholar (the name was omitted) also contained a similar offer.

Halevy had also given some thought to having the *Dorot Harishonim* translated into German.[50] Joseph Adler[51] had begun a translation of Volume Ic, which he had shown to Halevy. A German translation of a section of Volume Ic was published by his son, Samuel, in the *Jahrbuch* of the *Juedisch-Literarische Gesellschaft*.[52] A French translation of a section of Volume III appeared in the *Revue d'Etudes Juives*.[53]

Mention has been made of Halevy's scholarly followers who founded the *Juedisch-Literarische Gesellschaft* with him and published articles in accord with his views. Halevy followed their writings with paternal interest.[54] Nonetheless he regretted that he did not have enough disciples to whom he could impart his teachings and his views on subjects he considered important.[55]

Wolf Jawitz, in his letter[56] to Halevy as early as 1905, noted with regret that he was unable to incorporate Halevy's contributions to Jewish history in those volumes which had already been published. In the introduction to the sixth volume of his *Toledot Yisrael,* dated 5665 (1905), Jawitz lauded Halevy's historical defense of traditional Judaism. Thus beginning with this volume, embracing the era of Rabban Johanan ben Zakkai, Jawitz referred constantly to the *Dorot Harishonim* in his footnotes. Jawitz was overflowing with praise for Halevy in an article in the *Jahrbuch der Juedisch-Literarische Gesellschaft,*[57]

---

[49] Halevy Number 44.
[50] Halevy Number 45.
[51] *Sefer Zikaron Lerabbee Yitzhak Isaac Halevy,* pp. 83, 88.
[52] *"Ubersetzungsprobe zu Dorot Harishonim,"* XVII (1926), pp. 163-187.
[53] See above page 29.
[54] Halevy Number 125.
[55] *"Erinnerungen an Isaak Halevy,"* Der Israelit, June 4, 1914, p. 3.
[56] Halevy Number 10a.
[57] *"Neue juedische Geschichtsforshung und einige ihrer wichtigsten Resultate,"* IV (1906), pp. 283-292.

in which he concluded that the new historical discoveries of Halevy were in themselves an important historical event.

Binyamin M. Lewin[58] considered himself to be a disciple of Halevy and he spent many hours discussing his research with him. He referred to Halevy as an authority on the Oral Law.[59] Lewin and Aaron Hyman incorporated Halevy's studies on the *Igeret Rav Sherira Gaon* in their respective editions of the *Igeret*.[60]

It should be noted, however, that even Halevy's admirers could not overlook some weak points in his work.[61]

Beginning with 1904 the *Dorot Harishonim* was cited in the bibliographies of the Jewish encyclopedias and since 1910 Halevy has been listed in all the major Jewish encyclopedias as an Orthodox interpreter of Jewish history. A number of commentaries of Jewish classics have utilized the *Dorot Harishonim* as a major reference.[62] Some Jewish history text books lean upon Halevy's views.[63]

Halevy's volumes were not intended for popular reading. Aaron Hyman, an admirer of Halevy who incorporated Halevy's views in his own encyclopedic work listing the Talmudic sages, *Toledot Tannaim Veamoraim*, observed[64] that Halevy's writings were not easy to comprehend. This may account for the fact that neither Halevy's role in Jewish historiography nor his views

---

[58] "*Mitoldotai.*" *Sinai*, Adar-Nissan 5604, p. 196; — "*Devarim Ahadim*," introduction to *Dorot Harishonim*, VI, p. 9.

[59] Introduction to his edition of the *Igeret*, p. XVI.

[60] Introduction to Hyman's edition, p. 8; Introduction to Lewin's edition, p. XXXVII.

[61] M. Elias, *op. cit.*, p. 114.

[62] Such as Lewin's *Ozar Hageonim* and the Soncino English translation of the Babylonian Talmud.

[63] Moses Auerbach, *Toledot Am Yisrael;* Yaakov Gutkovsky, *Korot Am Olam;* Heimann Kottek, *Geschichte der Juden* (also in Yiddish translation); Meir Szczaransky, *Heavar Hayisraeli*.

[64] Introduction, p. 12.

are generally   known. However, the list of scholarly works
that refer to the *Dorot Harishonim* is growing steadily—some
utilizing it as a springboard for their own views.[65]

Special mention should be made of Mordecai (Markus)
Elias's essay[66] highlighting some of Halevy's major contributions to Jewish history and Meyer Waxman's section on Halevy
in his *History of Jewish Literature.*[67]

While Halevy had his reasons which led him almost single-
handedly into battle against the foremost historians, he, in
turn, became the target of a formidable list of critics. Some of
them[68] parenthetically acknowledged his greatness, nonetheless.
Undoubtedly, Halevy's sharp pen was an added factor that irked
many to retaliate in kind.[69]

Halevy's inordinate style of writing might have been a carry-
over from a number of classic rabbinical works. The com-
mentators alongside the *R. Alfasi* in the Vilna editions of the
Talmud Bavli, R. Zerahia Halevy (*Hamaor*) and R. Abraham
b. David (*Rabad*), used strong language in their disputations.[70]
Still stronger language may be found between R. Shlomo b.
Abraham (*Rashba*) and R. Aaron Halevy (*Reah*) in their
Mishmeret Habayit and *Bedek Habayit*, respectively. Thus
Halevy's correspondence relating to his own followers at times

---

[65] Such as Y. S. Zuri's *Shilton Haneseeut Vehavead*, III-1, pp. 8ff.

[66] *Op. cit.,* pp. 155-173.

[67] Vol. IV, pp. 720-727.

[68] E. Atlas in *Sefer Hashanah Shel Nahum Sokolov*, I, 5660, p. 102; Y. N.
Simhoni in *Hatekufah*, VI, 5681, p. 427.

[69] Thus a severly critical article on Halevy by I. Elbogen (*MGWJ*, 1902,
pp. 1-48) led A. Marx (*ZfHB*, 1902, p. 136) to remark: *"Kann ich mein
Bedauern nicht unterdruecken, dass Elbogen sich dazu hat hinreissen lassen, einen
ausserordentlich scharfen Ton gen Halevy anzuschlagen. Wenn man sich ueber
Halevy's Angriffe auf seine Vorgaenger entruestet, sollte man nicht in den gleichen
Fehler verfallen!"*

[70] Extant mss. of these texts indicate that the personality attacks in the printed
versions were toned down.

was penned in a tone which was similar to that reserved for the targets of his ire in the *Dorot Harishonim.*

Halevy was at ease in the rabbinical literature of his day, which was on the whole weak in form and style. However, he had a keen sense for such criteria in evaluating the writings of others.[71] Halevy's son[72] observed that his father's creativity was not hampered by literary birth pangs and that he wrote continuously when at his desk except for a short break for lunch.

Halevy confided to Rosenheim that in the course of his writing during the day he would rely mainly on his photographic memory when referring to the primary sources. Evenings he would check his material with the texts.

In a footnote in the *Dorot Harishonim,*[73] Halevy explained how some subject matter became clearer to him as his studies progressed which led him to a revision in his interpretation. The present writer also traced several changes in his interpretation of the Mishnah *Ediot* VII:7.[74]

In acknowledging a request for additional information on a topic in the *Dorot Harishonim,* Halevy pointed out[75] that although he covered his subjects adequately there would naturally be further elaboration of the subject matter in his forthcoming volumes.

Halevy's works contained many daring hypotheses that have been attacked particularly by those circles who were censured by him.[76] Many of the scholarly imputations leveled against him, however, were based on mere conjecture.

---

71 Halevy Number 29.
72 S. Halevy, *op. cit.,* p. 49.
73 Vol. Ie, p. 56.
74 See Hebrew edition of this volume.
75 Halevy Number 7a.
76 *Juedisches Lexikon,* II, p. 1360.

Thus Rudolf Leszynsky[77] accused Halevy of not utilizing the Greek texts of Josephus. However, the Halevy correspondence revealed[78] that he made use of the Greek text of *Antiquities* besides two German translations.[79] In the manuscript of the *Dorot Harishonim,* Volume Id,[80] Halevy likewise quoted from the Greek text of Josephus. He also studied[81] the *Chronicles* of Eusebius in the Latin.

Leszynsky also severely criticized Halevy for the manner in which he quoted from Josephus. What is most ironical is that in his very first item of criticism concerning Halevy's interpretation of the Pharisees as described by Josephus, Leszynsky's "unquestionable" interpretation is not universally accepted. Leszynsky[82] could not see how Halevy did away with the idea of the transfer of souls in Josephus's explanation of the Pharisees' beliefs. However, the scholarly Hebrew translator of Josephus, Y. N. Simhoni,[83] corroborated Halevy's interpretation.

Halevy felt[84] that it was beneath his dignity to reply to Leszynsky's unwarranted accusations.

As for Halevy's interpretive translations, Salomon Bamberger, who helped Halevy with the preparation of his Volumes Ic

[77] *"Isak Halevis Zitate,"* *Monatsschrift fuer die Geschichte und Wissenschaft des Judentums,* 1912, p. 568.

[78] Halevy Number 19.

[79] *Dorot Harishonim,* Ic, p. 86.

[80] Pp. 49-50. Also Halevy Number 60.

[81] Halevy Numbers 138, 139.

[82] *Op. cit.,* 568-569, translated a section of *Wars* II, 8, 14, *"Jede Seele unvergaenglich, aber nur die der Guten gehen in einen anderen Koerper ueber."* In light of this translation, Leszynsky noted: *"Mit klaren Worten schreibt Josephus also den Pharisaeern den Glauben an die Seelenwanderung . . . Wie aber uebersetzt Halevi [Dor. Har. Ic, p. 362] das unbequeme Zitat? 'Sie glauben, dass die Seelen saemtlich uebrig bleiben und dass die Seelen der Gerechten . . .' Halevi unterschlaegt seinen Lesern . . . die Seelenwanderung vollkommen."*

[83] *Kitvei Yoseph ben Matityahu — Toledot Milhemet Hayehudim,* Warsaw, 5683, p. 119.

[84] Halevy Number 154.

and Ie, noted[85] that part of his work was to compare Halevy's manuscripts with the quoted texts and to correct them accordingly. B. M. Lewin in editing Halevy's Volume VI[86] likewise compared Halevy's translation of Wellhausen with the original.

Halevy was conversant with those in Orthodox circles whose viewpoints differed from his. In the course of his response to a query of the Rabbi of Vienna, Moritz Guedemann,[87] Halevy recalled an earlier conversation wherein they did not agree with a number of his historical conclusions.

As for his outspoken contemporary critics, Halevy believed[88] that many of them would not have written so disparagingly of his works had they been more widely read. He observed[89] that the Hungarian scholars who deliberately disregarded his writings were under the strong influence of the reform elements in *hokhmat Yisrael.*

Halevy realized that his views would not be readily acknowledged by the non-Jewish scholars. When writing about his work to his son, Samuel,[90] who was studying in a Swiss University, Halevy resigned himself to the fact that the gentile professors would not accept his ideas.

Robert Travers Herford, a gentile scholar, writing on the Sadducees in the *Universal Jewish Encyclopedia,*[91] omitted Halevy in the bibliography. Nor did Herbert Danby in the introduction to his translation of *The Mishna*[92] list Halevy among the many

---

85 Introduction to Volume Ie.

86 Introduction, p. 10.

87 From Halevy letter in *Mee Natan Limesheesah Yaakov Veyisrael Labozezim,* by M.H.E. Bloch, p. 164.

88 Halevy Number 34.

89 Halevy Number 42b.

90 Halevy Number 129.

91 Vol. IX, pp. 308-309. In Herford's volume, *The Pharisees,* however, Halevy's views on the Sadducees were noted.

92 London: Oxford Press, 1933.

authorities on this subject. The notable exceptions were George
Foot Moore and Hermann L. Strack[93] in their respective monumental works, *Judaism in the First Centuries of the Christian
Era* (1927-1930) and *Einleitung in Talmud und Midrasch*
(1921). In his evaluation of Halevy, Strack[94] concluded that
"his all too sharp polemics [are] often materially in the right
. . . He has adherents and opponents equally passionate."

Meyer Waxman's[95] evaluation of Halevy's role in historiography is worthy of repetition:

> Halevy, in the long course of his discussion, corrected
> a large number of historical details in the works of earlier
> scholars . . . his extremism may serve as a check against
> views of scholars who veer in the opposite direction, and
> endeavor to minimize the force of continued tradition in
> Jewish history, making the complex Oral Law a result
> of haphazard causes and imaginary conditions. No new
> history of the ramified subject of the Oral Law can be
> written without consulting the work of Halevy.

[93] Strack informed Kottek (Halevy Number 82) that his utilization of the
Dorot Harishonim was limited since it was not indexed.

[94] *Introduction to the Talmud and Midrash*, p. 106.

[95] *A History of Jewish Literature*, Vol. IV, p. 727.

CHAPTER SIX

Halevy on the Sadducees

ALEVY'S ENLIGHTENING CONTRIBUTIONS to Jewish historiography can be fully appreciated only by following his train of thought and the manner in which he interpreted the sources in his polemics. A definitive resume of Halevy's writings which he had hoped to see published in his lifetime, is yet to be done.

The following is a distillation of Halevy's views on but one era of Jewish history which he considered of vital significance.

THEIR ORIGINS AND CREED

The Sadducean movement may be traced to the Hellenists with the disintegration of the priesthood in the days of Onias II.[1] As a result of his financial intrigues, Joseph the tax-collector allied himself with Hellenistic and Samaritan elements and became the forerunner of the Sadducess.

Joseph and his followers had no religious convictions.[2] His affinities to the priestly family accounted for the fact that the priests evolved among the Sadducean leaders.[3] Only later were historic and philosophic bases found for Sadduceeism by attributing its origin to the dictum of Antigonos.[4]

The Sadducees were essentially political opportunists.[5] During the pre-Hasmonean period their quest for sovereignty led them

---

[1] *Dorot Harishonim,* Ic, pp. 182, 374, 620.
[2] Ic, p. 184.
[3] Ic, p. 621 note.
[4] Ic, pp. 170-1.
[5] Ic, pp. 359, 367.

to become Hellenistic chauvinists.[6] Later, their interest in a state religion as an expediency for sovereignty, caused them to force circumcision even upon conquered heathens.[7] During the reign of the latter Hasmoneans, they were ready to abide by Pharisaic Law because they would not be tolerated otherwise.[8]

The Sadducees were not versed in the sources of the Law;[9] nor did they have historical roots for their interpretations of the Torah.[10]

The Sadducean members of the Sanhedrin in the days of the High Priests Johanan and Janai were not authorities in the Law and they relied upon secondary sources.[11] Hence their judging contrary to the acknowledged Law when they interpreted literally the "burning" of a priest's daughter (Leviticus 21:9).[12]

The earlier agitations of the Sadducees were political in nature. It was toward the close of their era that the Sadducean sect, the Boethusians, engaged the Pharisees in religious controversies.[13] Such differences are recorded in post-Talmudic sources as in the *Scholia* of the *Megilat Taanit*. The arguments mentioned in the Talmud likewise refer to their latter days before the destruction of the Temple.[14]

Since their adoption of the Law was only a matter of expediency, they had no formulated principle when they resorted to the literal interpretation of the Torah.[15] They maintained that unless the texts of the Torah were self explanatory, the individual

---

[6] Ic, pp. 184ff, 364ff.
[7] Ic, p. 393.
[8] Ic, p. 364.
[9] Ic, p. 412.
[10] Ic, pp. 430, 432.
[11] Ic, p. 464.
[12] Ic, pp. 412ff, 432; Ie, p. 13.
[13] Ic, pp. 419-21, 430-1.
[14] Ic, p. 432.
[15] Ic, pp. 368, 406, 415.

had the right to give his own interpretation to those texts which lent themselves to different meanings.[16] Thus their primarily utilitarian interpretations were incongruous at times even with the clear meaning of the texts as when they held the masters responsible for the damages of their slaves and in their promulgation of private financing of the daily sacrifices.[17] An apparent stand was taken by them primarily in the categories of laws where their political prestige was involved, such as in selected temple matters and official opinions emanating from the Sadducean dominated courts.[18]

The Sadducean view that the daily sacrifices could be offered with private funds had no recorded precedent.[19] The Sadducees were compelled to seek a religious basis for the private sponsorship of public sacrifices because they thereby had reason to release the Temple sacrificial funds for their own interests.[20] However since they did not wish to jeopardize the uninterrupted contributions for the sacrificial funds from the Jewish communities in the diaspora which were likewise under the influence of the Pharisees, the *status quo* was maintained as a Pharisaic victory.

The Pharisaic interpretation of *lex talionis* was not a later development of the Biblical Law or an improvement of the Sadducean literal explanation; rather it was evident from the text.[21] Since the Torah specifically forbade the monetary redemption of a murderer, the principle of redemption was implied in all other cases where *lex talionis* was expected. R. Eliezer who renders "eye for an eye" as actual, seemingly an opinion akin to the Sadducean view, is concerned with a halakhic detail relating

[16] Ic, p. 407.
[17] Ic, pp. 413-5.
[18] Ic, p. 411.
[19] Ic, 413, 448.
[20] Ic, pp. 28, 60, 449-50.
[21] Ic, pp. 425-6.

to the payment of the damage within the framework of the traditional interpretation, e.g. that payment must be in accordance with the worth of the eye of the perpetrator of the act and not of the victim.

The denial of such theological principles as the immortality of the soul, providence, God's concern in man's doing good or evil and eternal reward and punishment, predicated their disbelief of His omnipotence and of revelation.[22] The Sadducees observed the traditional Law only because that was the *sine qua non* for establishing their *raison d'etre* among the Jews.[23]

The conduct of Johanan Hyrcanus recorded in the Talmud (Kidushin 66a) evidenced the Sadducees' opposition to laws of rabbinical origin.[24] It was in order to insure his position as High Priest that Johanan upon the instigation of his Saducean circle issued an edict against Rabbinical Law. Thus he avoided any questions of Rabbinical Law regarding his qualifications for the priesthood. Were he to have rejected the traditional interpretation of the Biblical Laws, it would have meant the reconstruction of all Biblical Laws—and of this there is no trace. For the revision of the traditional character of the Torah would have required more than a formal proclamation. By this decree Johanan nonetheless helped strengthen the Sadducean influence in his reign.

HISTORICAL ASPECTS

The Hasmonean High Priests affiliated with the Sadducees were primarily concerned with state matters.[1] They officiated at

---

[22] Ic, pp. 326, 362-6.
[23] Ic, pp. 370, 373.
[24] Ic, pp. 391-3, 399-405, 438, 461.

[1] Ic, pp. 466-7.

public services in the Temple on Succot; of their number only Johanan officiated in the Holy of Holies on Yom Hakippurim.

Alexander Janai's levirate marriage to Alexandra was in conformity with Jewish Law, since it was consummated before he assumed the High Priesthood.[2] The difference in their ages (he was 22 and she was 37) would indicate that their marriage was the result of Aristobulus' death.[3]

With Janai's ascension to the throne, Alexandra was able to effect the return of her brother, Shimon ben Shetah, to the Court and the Sanhedrin.[4] Through skillful diplomacy, Shimon was able to restore gradually Pharisaic influence in the Sanhedrin.[5] Shimon also helped stem the tide of Sadducean influence among the people by innovating public elementary education through the auspices of Joshua ben Gamla.[6]

Queen Alexandra's role in protecting the Pharisees was short lived, however, with the recurrent Sadducean domination of Janai's Court.[7]

Josephus' reference to a revolt of the Jews in the courtyard of the Temple, which was likewise recorded in the Mishnah, was in fact plotted by Janai.[8] Anticipating some protests that would most likely follow the actions of the Sadducees on the Temple grounds, Janai had engaged foreign troops to quell any disorders in the Temple area. Thus any attempt on the part of the Jews to assert themselves was immediately interpreted by the Sad-

[2] Ic, p. 458.
[3] Ic, p. 460.
[4] Ic, p. 461.
[5] Ic, pp. 462-4, 468, 475.
[6] Ic, pp. 464-7.
[7] Ic, p. 479.
[8] Ic, pp. 481-2.

ducees as rebellious.[9] In like manner was the "rebellion" in the time of Johanan.[10]

Janai's persecution of the Pharisees incited similar attacks on the Jews in other lands as well.[11]

The submissiveness of the Jews, however, brought upon them only further barbarous persecutions.[12] It was only after a series of such betrayals that the Jews finally revolted; to have endlessly submitted to the Sadducean mores would have been suicidal.[13]

Josephus' connotation of the term Pharisees with the leaders of the Jews, nonetheless, cannot exclude the people who followed the sages.[14] Not only were the Pharisees (leaders) opposed to Sadducean rule, but this opposition was shared by the Jews as an entity.[15]

The restoration of the Pharisaic rule, suggested by Janai on his death bed, was the only solution for the stability of the land. He was aware that only this change would satisfy the people and would ultimately save the Hasmonean House as well.[16]

The Jewish nation prospered after the death of Janai during Queen Alexandra's reign solely because of the Pharisaic leadership whose administrative and judicial positions were dedicated to the welfare of the people.[17] In contrast, the dominion of the preceding autocratic rulers was attained as a result of despotism and bloodshed.

Josephus by his meagre descriptions of this era did not do justice to the Torah aspects of the Jewish community nor to

[9] Ic, p. 487.
[10] Ic, pp. 518-9.
[11] Ic, p. 495.
[12] Ic, p. 493.
[13] Ic, pp. 486, 489.
[14] Ic, pp. 483, 612.
[15] Ic, p. 532.
[16] Ic, p. 503.
[17] Ic, pp. 509-10, 517, 618.

the beneficial effects of the Pharisaic leadership.[18] His interests were with the Sadducees and his degradation of the Pharisaic rule evidenced his prejudice against them.[19]

The punishment meted out by the Pharisees to the Sadducees who were responsible for Janai's crucifying the Jews, was an act of justice rather than irresponsible terror.[20] The Sadducees, however, took advantage of these persecutions to lay the groundwork for disrupting the *status quo* of the Pharisaic leadership, by threatening to join the enemies of the Jewish nation.[21] Shimon was already dead, and Alexandra, alone and aged, had to yield to the demands of the Sadducees for partial control of the country.[22] This ultimately ruined the peaceful State which the Pharisaic reign had established.[23]

With the return of Aristobulus II and the Sadducees, the people remained loyal to the Pharisees and did not give their allegiance to the new government.[24] Thus King Aretas easily entered Jerusalem without fearing Aristobulus' forces.[25] This Aretas did not dare do before when the Pharisees served as the backbone of the Jewish forces. Until this time the Jews, notwithstanding their difficulties, wished to preserve the House of the Hasmoneans. Contrary to Aristobulus' fear, it was only the Pharisees then who could have preserved the Hasmonean traditional role.[26]

The Pharisees were disengaged from the civil war between Aristobulus and Hyrcanus because justice and righteousness were

[18] Ic, pp. 521, 537.
[19] Ic, pp. 510, 693.
[20] Ic, pp. 512, 514, 521.
[21] Ic, pp. 523ff.
[22] Ic, p. 71.
[23] Ic, p. 525.
[24] Ic, p. 527.
[25] Ic, pp. 539-40.
[26] Ic, p. 542.

on neither side and they foresaw the danger of interference by the Roman Empire.[72]

To the lasting sorrow of the Jewish people the Sadducees acted selfishly and irresponsibly.[28] Because of their actions the high moral standards of the community were affected. Their leaders had no convictions and their actions were of no credit to the Jews.[29] Their leaders and High Priests exploited the Jews for personal interests.[30] The events surrounding the break of Johanan with his people is evidence of their lawlessness.[31]

Herod put an end to the Saducean role in the Jewish State during his reign since the Sadducees were associated with the House of Aristobulus, the foe of Hyrcanus and his father, Antipater.[32] Thus the Talmud does not mention them during the era of Hillel.

With the advent of the Roman regime, the Pharisees were in a position to re-establish the home rule of the Jews.[33] The Sadducees, nevertheless, made their reappearance.[34]

The ultimate fall of the Temple and decline of the Jewish State was attributed to the Sadducees by Josephus.[35]

After the destruction of the Temple the Sadducees detached themselves completely from Jewish life; they found their way, like Josephus and Agrippa, into the Roman aristocracy, and showed no concern for the persecuted Jews.[36]

Josephus' account of the War, intended for the Roman Court, was written mainly to justify the cause of Agrippa and his followers, to the further detriment of the defeated Jewish people, who were at the mercy of the Romans.[37]

---

[27] Ic, pp. 527-530, 541.

[28] Ic, pp. 446-7.

[29] Ic, pp. 516, 639; VI, p. 12.

[30] Ic, pp. 715-6; Ie, p. 8.

[31] Ic, p. 442.

[32] Ic, pp. 543-4.

[33] Ic, pp. 712, 714.

[34] Ic, p. 632; Ie, p. 8.

[35] Ie, pp. 4-6.

[36] Ie, pp. 39-40.

[37] Ie, p. 1.

CHAPTER SEVEN

Literati in His Correspondence

HEIMANN KOTTEK

ALEVY'S COPIOUS LETTERS to his bosom friend, Heimann Kottek, have brought to light the David-Jonathan lifelong bond that existed between them beginning with the turn of the twentieth century when Halevy spent his first two years in Germany in Bad Homburg and in the nearby city of Frankfurt.

Dr. Kottek, the Rabbi of Bad Homburg and a scholar in his own right, was an early admirer of Halevy. Kottek became his confidant and devoted co-worker when Halevy settled in Germany. Their relationship has become an open book through the extant collection of Halevy letters addressed to him dating from 1905 until 1912. If on the one hand Halevy was known to be captious minded in his *Dorot Harishonim,* on the other hand, through his correspondence with Kottek one discovers that Halevy had a capacity for friendship and warmth of a rare quality.

Halevy spent his summers in Bad Homburg as early as 1900 at Kottek's home.[1] After Halevy settled in Hamburg as *Klaus-rabbiner* in 1902, he continued his summer stays with Kottek. Kottek had rooms for rent[2] and Halevy was a paying guest.[3] Halevy would notify him well in advance of the dates of his arrivals.[4] He would always be back in Hamburg by *Succot.* (Those

[1] Halevy Number 4.
[2] Halevy Numbers 21, 152.
[3] Halevy Number 52.
[4] Halevy Numbers 13, 21, 52, 102, 103, 152.

years a train trip from Hamburg to Frankfurt, near Bad Homburg, took nine and one half-hours.) Halevy did not take Kottek's hospitality for granted as was indicated by his concern in one of his letters[5] to him asking whether his coming to Bad Homburg was not too much for the Kottek family. When Halevy had learned that Kottek was to visit Hamburg, he wrote to him[6] that it was assumed Kottek would stay at his home just like any close member of his family.

It was their mutual interests in the *Juedisch-Literarische Gesell-schaft* and the *Freie Vereinigung* that cemented their close relationship. Inasmuch as Kottek resided near Frankfurt where Halevy's *Dorot Harishonim* was being printed in 1906, Kottek was pleased to take care of the technical and financial arrangements in the preparation of the volume as well as in the distribution of the books.[7] Kottek's efforts did not go unappreciated.[8]

Halevy relied upon Kottek to supply him with various scholarly volumes that he needed for his research from a Frankfurt library.[9] These works were evidently not available in Hamburg where he resided. Halevy also depended upon Kottek to forward to him articles of significance in periodicals other than *Der Israelit* to which he already subscribed.[10]

Halevy's letters to Kottek employed an elaborate salutation an an expression of his high regard for him. While his frequent letters to Kottek were written in the usual Hebrew, Kottek's responses were written in German (Halevy quoted Kottek's very words in his correspondence in Hebrew transliteration).[11]

[5] Halevy Number 47.
[6] Halevy Number 68.
[7] Over forty letters deal wholly or in part with such matters.
[8] Halevy Number 24.
[9] Halevy Numbers 20, 40, 127.
[10] Halevy Number 58.
[11] Halevy Numbers 45, 153.

Since they wrote to each other frequently, Halevy expressed[12] brotherly concern in one of his letters when some time elapsed without his hearing from Kottek. Several days later he followed it up[13] with a prayer for his well-being. This personal anxiety was again evidenced by Halevy in another letter[14] some time thereafter.

Kottek leaned heavily upon Halevy's scholarly advice. Halevy recommended[15] revisions in his articles and suggested[16] source materials for his lectures. Halevy was also Kottek's authority on Jewish law. A number of Halevy's *responsa* were addressed to him.[17]

It was Halevy who convinced Kottek to write his textbook on Jewish history based on the *Dorot Harishonim*.[18] He encouraged him in this project by pointing out that once the work would get under way it would progress smoothly.[19] Halevy was in constant touch with Kottek about this project.[20] One of the reasons Halevy noted for cancelling a planned trip to Russia was his desire to help Kottek with this work.[21] Of interest was Halevy's advice to Kottek[22] to write objectively and without scorn on the subject of Moses Mendelssohn, the father of the *haskalah* (enlightenment) movement.

Kottek's resulting work, *Geschichte der Juden,* was not seen in print by either Halevy or Kottek since they had both died by the time it was published by the *Juedisch-Literarische Gesellschaft*

---

12 Halevy Number 65.
13 Halevy Number 66.
14 Halevy Number 151.
15 Halevy Numbers 60, 126.
16 Halevy Number 106.
17 See above page 33.
18 Halevy Numbers 83, 95.
19 Halevy Number 84.
20 Halevy Numbers 89, 95, 102, 120, 131.
21 Halevy Number 102.
22 Halevy Number 120.

in 1915. The introduction to this volume refers to the Halevy-Kottek relationship and to their idealistic motives in the creation of the work.

The *Geschichte der Juden* was translated into Yiddish in 1932 and was used as a textbook in the Beth Jacob Schools in Poland. Its adoption by the Beth Jacob must be attributed to its roots in the *Dorot Harishonim.*

Halevy helped to arrange the *shiddukh*[23] between Kottek's daughter, Jenia, and Moses Auerbach, who headed the *Freie Vereinigung's* school system in the Holy Land. In the course of the budding romance Halevy observed that it would be worth her while to follow Auerbach even to Australia. Subsequently, Halevy was happy to extend felicitations to Kottek upon the forthcoming wedding[24] and he rendered a decision that it was permissible to set a date for the wedding in the latter part of a Hebrew month.[25] Kottek, however, died on the twenty-first of Tevet, 5673 (the close of 1912), before his daughter's wedding. In the obituary for Kottek in *Der Israelit*[26] Halevy's close association with him was recorded for posterity.

DAVID ZVI HOFFMANN

Some interesting facets of Halevy's relationship with the renowned R. David Zvi Hoffmann[1] (1843-1921) have come to light in the Halevy correspondence.

As early as 1901 Hoffmann had favorably reviewed the two

---

23 Beginning with Halevy Number 85.
24 Halevy Number 153.
25 Halevy Number 155.
26 January 2, 1913, pp. 9-10.

1 He is listed in the *Universal Jewish Encyclopedia*, V, p. 407.

volumes of the *Dorot Harishonim* that had already been published.[2]

When Hoffmann was in Hamburg for the Bar Mitzvah celebration of his nephew[3] in early 1907, Halevy was elated that he had the opportunity to engage in conversation with him the entire Saturday afternoon and late into the night.[4] Halevy was particularly gratified to hear him praise the *Dorot Harishonim* as a stepping stone toward a new era in Jewish historiography. It was evident from their discussions that Hoffmann had read from cover to cover Halevy's Volume Ic that had appeared the year before. Halevy[5] was extremely pleased with Hoffmann's review of this work which appeared in the *Juedische Presse*[6] several months after their meeting. He remarked that no one else could write so intelligently about his work.

Halevy and Hoffmann, however, had their differences on several subjects. Concerning the redaction of the Mishnah a number of comparative studies of their respective viewpoints have been published.[7] Halevy alluded to Hoffmann's views in the *Dorot Harishonim*[8] but he did not mention his name.

On the subject of the Sanhedrin, Hoffmann had prepared an article for the *Jahrbuch* which was critical of Halevy's views in the *Dorot Harishonim*. Halevy had expected Hoffmann's rebuttal and he considered answering Hoffmann's comments in the same issue of the *Jahrbuch*.[9] Upon further reflection Halevy

---

[2] Vol. II: *ZfHB*, 1901, pp. 100-107; Vol. III: *"Ein Meisterwerk."* *Israelitische Monatsschrift-Wissenschaftliche Beilage zur Juedischen Presse*, Aug. 15, 1901.

[3] Mordecai Emanuel.

[4] Halevy Number 35.

[5] Halevy Number 42.

[6] 9 Iyar 5667.

[7] Jacob Herzog, *Mishnah Berakhot Peah Demai*, pp. VIII-XVIII; J. J. Weinberg, *"Leheker Hamishnah," Sefer Yovel Likhvod Shmuel Kalman Mirsky*, pp. 222ff.

[8] Weinberg, *ibid.*, p. 234.

[9] Halevy Number 58.

realized that an outright reply in his own name would lead to a countercharge by Hoffmann.[10] This battle among Orthodox scholars, he observed, would only bring joy to their common enemies. Halevy finally decided to have his rebuttal translated from the Hebrew into German in the form of an "editorial note."[11] Thus both articles appeared in the *Jahrbuch* of 1907-5668.[12] About a year later after the smoke cleared Halevy was still of the opinion that he was in the right.[13]

Nonetheless Halevy considered Hoffmann one of the contemporary giants in Jewish scholarship.[14]

WOLF JAWITZ

It was in 1905 that the historian, Wolf Jawitz, began to correspond with Halevy from Vilna.[1] Jawitz lauded Halevy's accomplishments in bringing to light the Jewish sources in Jewish historiography.[2] He pointed out that his own writings were in the same vein as Halevy's—a statement with which Halevy took exception on frequent occasions.

Jawitz mentioned in his first letter to him that he had to borrow the Halevy volumes from time to time. This was an indication that Jawitz was far from being in comfortable circumstances.

A year after Jawitz had written to Halevy, the latter had

---

[10] Halevy Number 59.
[11] Halvey Number 60.
[12] *"Bemerkungen zur Geschichte des Synedrion,"* von Rektor Dr. D. Hoffmann in Berlin, pp. 225-238; *"Nachbemerkung der Redaktion,"* pp. 238-244.
[13] Halevy Number 89.
[14] Halevy Number 154.

[1] Halevy Number 10a.
[2] See above pp. 54, 62.

occasion to refer to Jawitz in his correspondence.[3] While Halevy was critical of Jawitz's works on Jewish history, he nevertheless considered Jawitz the only one at the moment who was qualified to write a major history under the auspices of the *Juedisch-Literarische Gesellschaft* with his guidance. Since he felt that he was not getting his viewpoints across to Jawitz through the mail, Halevy arranged for Jawitz to visit him in Hamburg in order to discuss the subject matter thoroughly.

As a result of their meeting which lasted several days Jawitz decided to postpone the completion of his sixth volume of the *Toledot Yisrael* until the appearance of Volume Ic of the *Dorot Harishonim* so that he could utilize Halevy's views in the writings of the second half of his work.[4] Jawitz also promised to revise the introduction of that volume.

Halevy suggested that the *Gesellschaft* give a subvention to Jawitz for the publication of the sixth volume of the *Toledot Yisrael* providing that his suggestions would be followed. It was Halevy's wish that he be the only one to negotiate with Jawitz on behalf of the *Gesellschaft*. Halevy felt that his personal intervention was necessary since Jawitz, notwithstanding his piety, was under the influence of the antitraditional schools of Jewish history from his early days.

On the one hand, Halevy wrote to Jawitz[5] that he was pleased with his assurances that ultimately their "language would be one" in their approach to Jewish history. Accordingly, he promised to intervene with the *Juedisch-Literarische Gesellschaft* for his financial support. On the other hand, Halevy expressed[6] his doubts as to whether Jawitz would cooperate with him fully. Thus he did not wish to encourage Jawitz to leave Berlin for

[3] Halevy Number 17.
[4] Halevy Number 18.
[5] Halevy Number 18a.
[6] Halevy Number 26.

the Gesellschaft's center in Frankfurt until he would be convinced that Jawitz belonged there. The nature of the revisions that Jawitz would make in his sixth volume of the *Toledot Yisrael,* Halevy confided, would be the determining factor in reaching his decision.

When sections of Jawitz's revised volume reached Halevy in the spring of 1907, Halevy was keenly disappointed[7] that he had not succeeded in conveying his historical perspective to Jawitz. Although Jawitz proclaimed that he wrote in the spirit of Halevy's *Dorot Harishonim,* it did not appear so to Halevy. Halevy attributed Jawitz's inability to change his basic views to his early indoctrination by the German scholars (whom Halevy attacked in his own works) even though Jawitz's motives were noble.

To Halevy the saintliness of the *Tannaim* and the *Amoraim* was not subject to comparative studies nor did he consider it proper to make evaluations of their personalities.[8] He cited Jawitz's character studies of R. Hiya and R. Hanina[9] as typical of the "old school" of *hokhmat Yisrael.*

It was therefore no surprise to Halevy that the completed volume of 1907 did not live up to his expectations.[10] Halevy was also disturbed[11] that Jawitz did not give him proper credit in this volume for some of his original historical discoveries.

A short time thereafter when Halevy learned that Jawitz had requested a subvention for his forthcoming Volume VII of the *Toledot Yisrael,* he voiced disapproval.[12] He was quick to point out that he took care not to criticize Jawitz publicly, but did

[7] Halevy Number 39.
[8] *Dorot Harishonim,* Ie, pp. 372-373.
[9] *Toledot Yisrael,* VI, p. 255.
[10] Halevy Number 48.
[11] Halevy Number 47b.
[12] Halevy Number 59.

so through his personal correspondence. His bone of contention again was that Jawitz was unable to break away from the influences of Graetz and I. H. Weiss, and that all his efforts to counteract this approach from the very first time that he had written to Jawitz in Russia were in vain.[13]

While Halevy was not in favor of having the *Gesellschaft* subsidize the forthcoming volumes of the *Toledot Yisrael* because of his negative reactions to the sixth volume, the first edition of Jawitz's seventh volume published in Berlin in 1909 and the eighth volume published in Berlin in 1912 acknowledged the aid of the *Juedisch-Literarische Gesellschaft*.

Several years later when Jawitz made another request to the *Gesellschaft* for a subvention for a different kind of work, Halevy strongly urged that no further monies be advanced to Jawitz for his publications until they would be approved.[14] Nonetheless he followed up his strong remarks the very next day with a plea that his statement should not be circulated lest it be misunderstood as a personal feud.[15]

Even though Halevy possessed an uncompromising attitude in religious principles, yet his mind could be influenced by his sympathetic heart. Thus his correspondence revealed a personal concern regarding Jawitz's financial difficulties.[16] He was also on the alert for funds from various other sources for Jawitz.[17]

It was during the early negotiations relating to the *Toledot Yisrael* that Halevy was informed of Jawitz's plans to write a textbook with a "seminarist," which led him to make some caustic comments.[18] Another idea of Jawitz at the time which

---

[13] M. Szczaransky, *Heavar Hayisraeli*, I, p. 18, likewise noted that Jawitz did not grasp Halevy's approach in his historical writings.

[14] Halevy Number 122.

[15] Halevy Number 123.

[16] Halevy Numbers 34, 35, 36, 41.

[17] See also Elias, *op. cit.*, p. 158.

[18] Halevy Number 28.

did interest Halevy was a translation into German of Jawitz's own history.[19] After giving the matter further thought, however, Halevy came to the conclusion that this was not a project for the *Gesellschaft*.[20]

While the Halevy correspondence did not spell out all the reasons for his negative attitude towards Jawitz,[21] there were others within the *Gesellschaft*[22] who took issue with Jawitz on grounds similar to those that had been voiced by Halevy. Other religious circles have also been sensitive to his digressions from some traditional interpretations.[23]

Jawitz, even in the wake of Halevy's criticism, is nonetheless one of the staunchest spokesmen of the traditional school of Jewish historiography.[24]

JACOB ROSENHEIM

Halevy developed a warm friendship with Jacob Rosenheim by 1908 vis-a-vis their mutual interests in Jewish communal affairs that ripened with the passage of time. Rosenheim's name first appeared in the Halevy correspondence in regard to the controversial subject of Ahron Marcus.[1] Rosenheim considered Marcus one of his spiritual mentors[2] and tried to use his influence to have him appointed to a post within the *Juedisch-*

[19] Halevy Number 33.
[20] Halevy Numbers 38, 39.
[21] S. Halevy, *op. cit.,* pp. 55-59.
[22] Halevy Numbers 39, 66.
[23] M. Elias, *op. cit.,* p. 163; M. Waxman, *op. cit.,* pp. 730, 732.
[24] M. Elias, *ibid.,* p. 172; Yehoshua J. Preil, *Ketavim Nivharim,* I, (New York, 5684), p. 279.

[1] See above p. 50.
[2] Rosenheim, *op. cit.,* pp. 42-44.

Literarische Gesellschaft. Halevy, however, strongly objected[3] to any such association.

When Halevy first became involved with the *Freie Vereini-gung's* activities in the Holy Land he wrote to Kottek[4] requesting that Rosenheim clarify certain matters. In that letter he asked Kottek to point out to Rosenheim a correction in his quote of a Talmudic dictum as well as in some fact relating to the Russian rabbinate in one of his lead articles in *Der Israelit* (Rosenheim was its publisher).

Since Rosenheim was thirty-seven when he began his close association with Halevy, then sixty, it is quite evident that Halevy was the master and Rosenheim the disciple. By the end of 1908 Halevy noted[5] that he was corresponding with Rosen-heim almost daily. Rosenheim[6] recalled his wife handing to him one of Halevy's frequent letters and remarking, "Mazel tov! Another letter from your *kallah* (betrothed)." While Halevy's letters to Rosenheim were written in Hebrew, the salutations were consistently in Latin script, "Herrn Jacob Rosenheim."

Halevy's creative role in the *Freie Vereinigung* and subsequently in the founding of the Agudath Israel movement as unfolded in the pages of this volume, was sustained in great measure by Rosenheim.

SAMUEL HALEVY

Halevy's son, Samuel, was his close disciple. Samuel had planned to study at the University of Zurich[1] but he transferred

---

3 Halevy Numbers 37a, 52.
4 Halevy Number 52.
5 Halevy Number 84.
6 *Op. cit.,* p. 115.

1 Halevy Number 26b.

to Bern after a month because circumstances there made it difficult for him to get a good start.[2] Kottek was helpful by
providing him with some documents relating to the necessary
classical languages.[3] Halevy assisted Samuel with material for
his dissertation[4] and followed his progress with interest.[5] He
also advised him[6] how to go about its publication, which was a
prerequisite for the doctoral degree. Halevy had to intervene
with the editorial staff of the *Jahrbuch* of the *Juedisch-Literarische Gesellschaft* in order to assure its publication therein
within the time required by the university.[7] He was particularly
proud of his son's scholarly work because it reflected his own
views.[8] Halevy acknowledged[9] Kottek's efforts in having Samuel's
thesis printed in the *Jahrbuch.* It was published under the title,
"Ist der Name 'juedischer Hellenismus' berechtigt?"[10] The title
of his dissertation for the university was not the same in defer-
ence to the wishes of his professor.[11]

The letters that Halevy wrote to his son were replete with
fatherly criticism and advice. He urged him to become a Swiss
citizen while a student there and suggested he should rent his
room in advance for the coming semester.[12] It was not beyond
him to remind Samuel to bring along his identification papers
for the police so that he should not have any difficulties at the
German border.[13] When Samuel was hospitalized, having become

---

[2] Halevy Number 27.
[3] Halevy Number 25.
[4] Halevy Number 107.
[5] Halevy Number 121.
[6] Halevy Number 129.
[7] Halevy Numbers 142, 144, 147 148.
[8] Halevy Number 148.
[9] Halevy Number 149.
[10] Vol. IX, (1911), pp. 421-489.
[11] Halevy Number 147.
[12] Halevy Number 67.
[13] Halevy Number 108.

critically ill with pneumonia during the spring of 1912, Halevy took it very much to heart.[14]

Samuel had started a biography of his distinguished father, a tribute to Halevy's code of honor and integrity that only a son could observe at close range. Excerpts of a Hebrew translation of this unfinished work which had been written in German were published in 1964 in the memorial volume, *Sefer Zikaron Lerabbee Yitzhak Isaac Halevy*,[15] commemorating Halevy's fiftieth *yahrzeit*.

Samuel married Rekha, the daughter of Shlomo Jacobson of Hamburg. The couple moved to Leipzig where Samuel was associated with an insurance firm. Afterward they settled in Israel. Samuel died in 1943. Samuel's two sons, Isaac and Moshe, as well as his three daughters, all married, reside in Israel.

OTHER LITERATI

Halevy's correspondence abounds with comments about a number of other renowned personalities in Jewish scholarship.

Halevy was aware of Ismar Elbogen's abusive criticism of his views.[1] It was his conviction[2] that Elbogen was primarily concerned with the defense of the Graetz school despite his objective criticism.

Halevy was likewise vexed[3] by Baer Ratner's[4] attacks on the *Dorot Harishonim*.[5] He noted that another critic, Samuel Abra-

---

[14] Halevy Number 149.
[15] *"Avee Zikhrono Liverakha,"* pp. 13-63.

[1] See above p. 64, note 69.
[2] Halevy Number 76.
[3] Halevy Number 21.
[4] He is listed in the *Universal Jewish Encyclopedia*, IX. p. 84.
[5] A series appeared in *Hamelitz*, 5660.

ham Poznanski, took Ratner to task for his impropriety in his criticism. Thus when Ratner was about to submit an article for the *Jahrbuch* of the *Juedisch-Literarische Gesellschaft,* Halevy drafted[6] a reply in the German language (in Hebrew script) for the *Gesellschaft* rejecting his offer. He pointed out that while the *Jahrbuch* welcomed objective scholarly works, it could not accept the writings of those concerned only with defending the Frankel-Graetz schools without regard for the *Dorot Harishonim.*

Halevy, sensitive about his scholarly reputation, resented an anonymous review of his work which appeared in the *Frankfurter Israelitisches Familienblatt.*[8] He attributed it to Ahron Marcus. In it Abraham Harkavy was singled out for his modernity and progressiveness in contrast with Halevy. He was particularly disturbed that the author did not acknowledge his Talmudic erudition as being superior to Harkavy's.

In answer to such critics as Abraham Epstein[9] who took Halevy to task for referring only to the *Sefer Hayuhsin* edition of the *Igeret Rav Sherira Gaon* in his studies on the *Saboraim* in Volume III of the *Dorot Harishonim,* Halevy reiterated his views to his son[10] relating to the chronology in his original work. Subsequently Halevy noted[11] that B. M. Lewin's study of various manuscripts of the *Igeret* which he was collecting throughout Europe confirmed Halevy's point that the *Yuhsin* edition was the principal one. Halevy was in favor of having the *Juedisch-Literarische Gesellschaft* associated with Lewin's work on the *Igeret.*[12]

---

[6] Halevy Number 21.

[7] Halevy Number 42.

[8] *"Doroth Harischonim,"* April 26, 1907, p. 9, *et. seq.*

[9] *Igerot Bikoret,"* Haeshkol V, 5665, p. 256.

[10] Halevy Number 76.

[11] Halevy Number 99.

[12] It was published with the assistance of the *Gesellschaft* in Haifa, 1921.

Halevy was gratified to learn[13] that a newly discovered *Epistle of Rabbenu Hushiel* among the *Genizah* in Oxford confirmed his contention[14] that the "Four Captives" came from Italy. He urged[15] Kottek to publish an article regarding this discovery and to refer to a previous article he had written on this very subject in defense of Halevy. Halevy was also interested in having the *Gesellschaft* acquire this manuscript.[16]

Halevy was convinced[17] that the *Seder Kadashim* of the *Talmud Yerushalmi* which appeared in 1906 was a forgery. Accordingly he cautioned Kottek against having this work reviewed in the *Jahrbuch.* An anonymous article in *Der Israelit*[18] voicing this idea might have come from Halevy's pen.

Halevy had little regard for the views of the non-Jewish scholars, Karl Marti[19] and Bernhard Stade.[20] Halevy's son, Samuel, in the course of preparing his doctoral dissertation under Marti, a professor at the University of Bern, related to his father some of Marti's criticism on the subject of Hellenism in light of the *Dorot Harishonim.* Halevy, in turn, pointed out[21] where Marti had erred. Nonetheless he realistically advised his son not to refer to the *Dorot Harishonim.* He likewise brought to Samuel's attention[22] some additional material to refute Stade's views, which he urged him to incorporate in an article in the *Jahrbuch* contra Stade.

The Jewish historical work, *Hikrei Lev-Seder Dorot Hatanaim*

---

13 Halevy Number 30.
14 *Dorot Harishonim,* III, pp. 283ff.
15 Halevy Number 31.
16 Halevy Number 34.
17 *Idem.*
18 "*Zum Jerushalmi* (?) *Seder Kodaschim,*" Aug. 15, 1907, pp. 11-12.
19 Listed in *Universal Jewish Encyclopedia* VII, p. 385.
20 Listed in *Jewish Encyclopedia* XI, p. 525.
21 Halevy Number 129.
22 Halevy Number 67.

Veamoraim,[23] by Yehuda Leib Landesberg, did not rate high
with Halevy.[24] Recognizing his writing ability, however, Halevy
invited him in the name of the *Juedisch-Literarische Gesellschaft*[25]
to undertake under its sponsorship the preparation of a history
based on the *Dorot Harishonim.*

Halevy took notice[26] of the fact that the *Dor Yesharim* by
R. Yehuda Lipschitz[27] of Russia, a work in defense of the Oral
Law, acknowledged the significant role of the *Dorot Harishonim.*
Halevy considered it worthwhile especially for the younger rabbis
and the reading circles in Russia as a proper introduction to this
subject. Nonetheless he had some reservations about its scholarly
style.[28] It required some effort on his part to see to it that the
Juedisch-Literarische Gesellschaft grant the publisher of the two
volumes modest subventions.[29]

Halevy[30] considered the *halakhic* work, *Besamim Rosh,* falsely
attributed to the *Rishon* R. Asher b. Yehiel. He pointed out that
the reason the renowned R. Ezekiel Landau, author of the
Noda Biyehuda, did not counteract it was simply because the
work appeared the year he died in 1793, when he was already
incapacitated. A section of this work was subjected to the acid
test by Halevy in the *Dorot Harishonim.*[31] Among the Halevy
correspondence[32] were also some comments on the *Amoraim,* R.
Joseph, Ravina, R. Papa, and R. Huna.

---

23 Part I, Satmar, 5665.   24 Halevy Numbers 39, 62, 66.

25 Halevy Number 42a. While Halevy Number 42a did not mention the
addressee (for that matter the name, Landesberg, did not appear in all of the
Halevy correspondence), Halevy's notation "Czeghalom" in the margin of Halevy
Number 42c, which is correlated to Halevy Number 42a, led to the determination
of his name — since the Rabbi of Szeghalom, Hungary, was Landesberg (S. N.
Gottlieb's *Oholei Shem,* p. 428); and the concomitant correspondence reveals that
he was in contact with this author of the *Hikrei Lev.*

26 Halevy Number 55.   27 See above p. 56.
28 Halevy Numbers 55, 120.   29 Halevy Numbers 59, 62, 63, 66.
30 Halevy Number 127.   31 Vol. Ie, pp. 120-121.
32 Halevy Number 44.

CHAPTER EIGHT

Freie Vereinigung

O NE OF THE MOVEMENTS on the German scene that attracted Halevy was the *Freie Vereinigung fuer die Interessen des orthodoxen Judentums* (Free Association for the Interests of Orthodox Judaism). This organization was formed by R. Samson Raphael Hirsch in 1885 in Frankfurt in order to strengthen the slender structure of Orthodoxy in his day and so enable it to rise to prominence in Jewish circles.[1] It served as mouthpiece for the spiritual and political interests of traditional Judaism through its publication of the *Mitteilungen.*

In 1907 the *Freie Vereinigung* was reorganized to embrace the interests of Orthodox Jews in all of Germany. Joining with the Frankfurt forces were such personalities as Meier Hildesheimer of Berlin, Isaac Auerbach and Benjamin Hirsch of Halberstadt, and Hermann Gumpertz, the renowned communal leader of Hamburg. R. Salomon Breuer was elected president of the *Vereinigung* and Jacob Rosenheim served as its executive vice-president.[2]

Halevy followed the development of the revitalized *Vereinigung* with keen interest.[3] It was his hope that Breuer would be able to meet the challenges of this organization. Halevy already had in mind some projects of his own that he hoped to carry out through its offices—its religious educational activities in the Holy Land were meant to be the first major step.

---

[1] H. Schwab, *History of Orthodox Jewry in Germany,* p. 89.

[2] In Rosenheim's autobiography, *Zikhronot,* pp. 34-134, the history of the *Freie Vereinigung* was recorded by one who was part of it.

[3] Halevy Number 49.

When Halevy was invited by Rosenheim to participate in a conference of the *Vereinigung* in Frankfurt, Halevy suggested[4] that it begin early in the week so that he could be back in Hamburg at his *Klaus* for the Sabbath. He noted further that if circumstances would require him to remain in Frankfurt on the Sabbath he would do so because there was not a thing that he would not do for the sake of Torah in *Eretz Yisrael.*

At the turn of the century there were already networks of schools in the Holy Land sponsored by the *Alliance Israelite Universelle*[5] and the *Hilfsverein der deutschen Juden.*[6] In these schools, however, preference was given to secular subjects. Even the languages of instruction until 1910 were French and German, respectively, while Jewish subjects were held down to a bare minimum.[7] To counteract this situation a network of Talmud Torahs had been organized by the *Shomrei Torah* Society in the Holy Land, emphasizing a religious program. The *Freie Vereinigung* had also established a school in Petah Tikvah in 1906. After its reorganization in 1907, the *Vereinigung's* expanding educational activities in the Holy Land gradually encompassed the *Shomrei Torah* sponsored schools whose financial structure was already in dire circumstances.[8]

Halevy had taken special notice[9] of a series of articles by R. Joseph Carlebach in *Die Juedische Presse* entitled, *"Der 'Issur' gegen die Schulen in Palestina,"*[10] which dealt with a sensitive aspect of religious education in the Holy Land. Carlebach, at

---

[4] Halevy Number 54.

[5] *Universal Jewish Encyclopedia,* I, p. 191.

[6] *Op. cit.,* V, p. 361.

[7] M. Blau, *Al Homotayikh Yerushalayim,* p. 48.

[8] *Die Freie Vereinigung fuer die Interessen des orthodoxen Judentums und Erez Jisroel,* Folge I, p. 10; Rosenheim, *op. cit.,* p. 94.

[9] Halevy Number 58.

[10] September 20, 1907, *et seq.;* N. Carlebach, *Joseph Carlebach and His Generation,* pp. 41-54.

the age of twenty-two, left Germany to teach mathematics and natural sciences at the Laemel Teacher's Seminary in Jerusalem. Upon his return to Germany three years later in 1907 he was reprimanded by some religious circles for having taught there since some rabbis in the Holy Land had placed a ban on the institution. In the aforementioned article Carlebach reviewed the course he had taken. The seminary was founded with the understanding that it would operate in strict accord with Jewish tradition. In his capacity as Chief Rabbi of Jerusalem, the *Hakham Bashi* called together a number of leading personalities who voted to approve the institution. Many rabbis of Eastern European descent, however, were concerned lest the opening of a secular institution for training teachers would bring about an assimilation movement in the Holy Land similar to that which engulfed many Jewish communities in Europe under the influence of the emancipation. Accordingly, they placed a ban on the seminary. Carlebach pointed out that Jerusalem at that time did not have a central religious authority whose decisions would have been binding upon all Jews regardless of the country from which they had come. Thus R. Abraham I. Kook and R. David Friedman of Karlin declared that the ruling was binding only upon those who submitted to it of their own free will. It should be noted that prior to the establishment of the Laemel Teacher's Seminary some pious parents had been compelled to send their children to Christian missionary schools simply because there was no Jewish institution at which they could have received secular training.

Halevy's formal association with the *Freie Vereinigung* began in Heshvan 5668 (1907) when he was invited by Rosenheim and Jacob Strauss[11] to become a member of its Commission on

---

[11] Rosenheim, *op. cit.*, pp. 86 and 93, refers to him.

Literature and Publicity.[12] Shortly after accepting this invitation, he was asked to join the Palestine Commission to be headed by Rosenheim.[13] Halevy's main interest, however, was in another pending appointment as chairman of a subcommittee relating to the educational activities in the Holy Land, which was closer to his heart. He anticipated the appointment to its chairmanship. When he learned that it was to be named "Torah Commission," he pointed out[14] that this title would limit the effectiveness of the Commission in its negotiations with such organizations as the *Alliance, Hilfsverein,* Jewish Colonization Association[15] and the Zionists; these would likely claim that they had no concern for Torah education per se. Halevy therefore suggested the title Cultural Commission, which would compel the other organizations to accept it as their counterpart with many problems similar to theirs. As such they would have to deal with him as its representative in an official relationship. Herein was another illustration of the master strategist, Halevy, looking beyond the present. Thus a year after he had spelled out this suggestion there were allusions in Halevy's correspondence to negotiations with the *Alliance.*

Halevy also played a vital role in the *Vereinigung's* Commission on East European Jewry, which was duly acknowledged by Rosenheim.[17]

Halevy took his appointments in the *Freie Vereinigung* very seriously. As a member of the Commission on Literature and Publicity, he was invited to participate in its deliberations at the *Vereinigung's* conference that was to be held in Berlin

---

[12] Halevy Number 57.
[13] Halevy Number 58.
[14] Halevy Number 59.
[15] *Universal Jewish Encyclopedia,* **VI**, p. 97.
[16] Halevy Number 95.
[17] *Op. cit.,* p. 94.

beginning December 25, 1907. His creative mind would not permit him to be passive when he felt that the plans of that commission were floundering.[18] He was primarily interested, however, in the development of the Palestine Commission.

When Halevy heard that Kottek and Bamberger were hesitating to travel to Berlin, Halevy appealed[19] to them to change their minds. Halevy stressed the *Vereinigung's* great potentialities at this first assemblage of a united Orthodoxy in Germany. He felt, therefore that it was their moral duty to attend this event. *En passant* he pointed out some of the shortcomings of the forthcoming conference and noted how he helped make the program more meaningful by recommending that its agenda include the problem of the colonies in the Holy Land.

The proceedings of that conference[20] subsequently noted that Halevy was chairman of a subcommittee of the *Palestina-Kommission der Freien Vereinigung* whose purpose was to promote religious education in the "colonies" or settlements. Halevy was credited with launching the *Vereinigung's* educational activities in the Holy Land and with encouraging the placement of rabbis in the settlements.

Halevy's enthusiastic report[21] to Kottek who was unable to attend the conference, revealed his satisfaction with his role in the Palestine Commission. Now he was sanctioned to proceed with his long dormant projects for the Holy Land. His first step in his new capacity was to write to Jerusalem and Jaffa for certain information in order to orientate himself with the entire framework of religious education there. He was also concerned with the proper timing of the publicity for his programs so that the maximum benefit would be derived from them.[22]

[18] Halevy Number 60.
[19] Halevy Number 61.
[20] *Die Freie Vereinigung,* op. cit., pp. 6-9.
[21] Halevy Number 62.
[22] Halevy Number 63.

Halevy was personally acquainted from his Vilna days with many of the rabbis who were in the Holy Land at that time. Among them were Haim Berlin, Joseph Haim Sonnenfeld, Barukh Braverman and the Rabbi of Slutzk who resided in Safed.[23]

In a letter[24] addressed to the rabbinical leaders of the *Shomrei Torah* Society in Jerusalem, Halevy submitted a questionnaire concerning their schools in the colonies including enrollment problems, curriculum, faculty, students, rabbis in the colonies, tuition and finances. He prefaced his request with a report of the Commission's founding at the Berlin Conference. He concluded with the suggestion that their signatures be affixed to their reply. Two and one-half months later he accordingly received a letter from Jerusalem signed by the rabbis.[25]

In the summer of 1908 Halevy wrote again to the rabbinical heads of the *Shomrei Torah* Society[26] advising them that he had received two letters from Haifa requesting aid for their Talmud Torah and for the maintenance of their newly appointed rabbi. Halevy considered the matter of particular urgency because it involved a new community in the Holy Land and he followed up the matter the very same day. He informed them that the *Freie Vereinigung* would make up the entire deficit with the understanding that they engage a qualified instructor in Talmud and that provisions would be made for all who wished to attend. He suggested that their rabbi also supervise the Talmud Torah. There was one condition to the offer — the pupils over the age of nine should be taught the language of the land, Arabic or Turkish. The language teacher was to be a religious Jew, or if none were available, a non-Jew. In engaging another instructor

23 Halevy Number 77.
24 Halevy Number 64.
25 Halevy Number 71.
26 Halevy Number 81.

for the Talmud Torah he suggested they consider one who would inspire adults as well as the young. Halevy further requested that their acknowledgment be signed by one of the prominent rabbis so that the arrangement would be considered binding.

Of interest is that the rabbis of Jerusalem agreed to the provision permitting the study of "the language of the land."[27]

During this period Halevy entered into an extensive correspondence with R. Abraham I. Kook[28] who resided in Haifa, relating primarily to religious education and the religious structure of the colonies.[29] Halevy arranged to have one of Kook's letters translated into German for circulation among the members of the *Eretz Yisrael* Commission as well as for the public.[30] One of the committee's sessions was dedicated mainly to Kook's views, with Halevy and Rosenheim among the enthusiastic participants.[31]

R. Kook attempted to enlist Halevy's aid in the establishment of his central Yeshiva in the Holy Land. Halevy agreed with him that the time was ripe for launching rabbinical seminaries for young men in the Holy Land.[32] However, he believed that there was an immediate need for the placement of qualified spiritual leaders in the growing settlements in order that their religious communal character be safeguarded. Halevy foresaw Kook as the logical personality to serve as *Rav Hagalil* over the local rabbis.

Halevy[33] discerned the emergence of the Ashkenazic community in Jerusalem to the foremost position. He also saw the necessity for the establishment of a Chief Rabbinate.[34] Thus Halevy would

[27] Halevy Number 82.

[28] Eight letters from Kook to Halevy from 1908 to 1910 were published in the former's *Igerot Hareiyah*, numbers 103, 111, 137, 146, 149, 163, 203 and 272.

[29] Halevy Numbers 80a, 81.

[30] Halevy Number 73a.

[31] Reported by Binyamin M. Lewin in a letter to Kook.

[32] Rosenheim, *op. cit.*, p. 94.

[33] Halevy Number 43.

[34] Halevy Number 93.

have been the least surprised if he had been alive in 1919 to see R. Kook called to Jerusalem to become the Rabbi of all the Ashkenazic communities united under the *Vaad Hakelali,* and in 1921, elected Chief Rabbi of Palestine and head of the High Rabbinical Court. Nor was it suprising to find R. Kook heartily encouraging Halevy in his activities through the *Freie Vereinigung* in behalf of the Holy Land.[35]

At the start of Halevy's affiliation with the *Freie Vereinigung* its budget was very limited. Halevy[36] turned down Rosenheim's suggestion that he, Bamberger, Bondi and Kottek raise funds privately, insisting that all monies must be channeled through the *Vereinigung* in order that it maintain its organizational image. The Halevy correspondence leaves no doubt that Halevy was in charge of the projects in the Holy Land. The problem of finances, however, was in Rosenheim's lap.[37]

Halevy followed the activities of the *Vereinigung* regularly with his usual thoroughness.[38] When the *Hilfsverein der Deutschen Juden* proposed to join with the Orthodox forces in in the field of education in the Holy Land, Rosenheim referred the matter to Halevy.[39] The latter hastened to reply during *Hol Hamoed* (when writing is permitted under extreme urgency) that he was in favor of the *Hilfsverein's* offer on the condition that the *Vereinigung* would have full control over the appointments and salaries of the teachers and other such items. Amidst the negotiations, the *Hifsverein's* vice-president, Paul Nathan,[40] journeyed to the Holy Land. Rosenheim urged Halevy to write at once to the rabbis of Jerusalem and Jaffa advising them to clear any actions with Nathan through the *Vereinigung,* which ulti-

---

35 Kook, *op. cit.,* p. 212.
36 Halevy Number 72.
37 Rosenheim, *op. cit., pp.* 104-5.
38 Halevy Number 71.
39 Halevy Number 74.
40 He is listed in the *Universal Jewish Encyclopedia,* VIII, p. 110.

mately meant Halevy. Halevy also wrote to R. Kook[41] regarding the Paul Nathan matter.

Towards the end of 1908 plans were already under way by Halevy and Rosenheim for expanding the *Freie Vereinigung's* activities in Ekron, Rehovot, Rishon LeZion and Petah Tikvah through the *Shomrei Torah* Society schools.[42] By the spring of 1909, however, the school system which the *Shomrei Torah* Society had established was entirely supported by the *Vereinigung*,[43] and was now named, at the instance of Halevy, *Netzah Yisrael* (the eternity of Israel).[44] Later on this system also embraced the Sephardic Talmud Torah, *Doresh LeZion*, in Jerusalem.

Halevy took an active part in interviewing the candidates to teach in the Holy Land and in briefing those who were chosen.[45] He was also on the lookout for additional capable instructors.

Halevy's interest in religious education was not limited to his own *Netzah Yisrael* system.[46] He was ready to review with Dr. Joseph Engel, who was about to join the staff of the Tahkemoni school in Jaffa, such varied subjects as that school's relationship with the community and teachers of the *Gymnasium*.[47]

Halevy also had his share of frustration within the framework of the *Freie Vereinigung's* activities. Its representative in the Holy Land, Jonathan Benjamin Horowicz,[48] who was sent there without Halevy's blessings, proved to complicate matters by his independent actions.[49]

[41] Halevy Number 73a.
[42] Halevy Numbers 82, 84.
[43] Halevy Number 93.
[44] *Die Freie Vereinigung, op. cit.,* p. 21.
[45] Dr. Markus Elias was interviewed by Halevy before he left for the Holy Land in 1910 to teach. Dr. B. M. Lewin was also among the *Netzah Yisrael* instructors in 1912.
[46] Halevy Number 92.
[47] Halevy Number 95.
[48] Rosenheim, *op. cit.,* pp. 94-96, 104; *Die Freie Vereinigung, op. cit.,* pp. 9-11.
[49] Halevy Numbers 72, 91.

A significant step by the *Freie Vereinigung* was the appointment of Moses Auerbach to head its educational network in
Petah Tikvah.[50] It was Halevy who formally notified the *Roshei
Hamoshavah* of Petah Tikvah and R. Haim Berlin[51] of Auerbach's
appointment. He likewise sent a confirming letter to R. Kook on
this appointment.[52] Before leaving for the Holy Land, Auerbach
met with Halevy in connection with his new post.[53] He had a
high regard for Auerbach's ability and was very pleased with his
accomplishments there.

By 1910 the activities of the *Netzah Yisrael* schools flourished
so that there was need to engage an assistant to Auerbach.[54] In
1913 the *Netzah Yisrael* system encompassed ten schools, forty
teachers, and one thousand pupils. An additional school for
girls in *Petah Tikvah* was also sponsored by the Frankfurt
community.[55]

The *Shomrei Torah* Society was not out of the picture entirely.
In 1912 Halevy[56] discerned that there was an element in the
Holy Land interested in having some of the schools returned to
the *Shomrei Torah.*

Rosenheim was convinced that the pioneering activities of the
Orthodox Jews were the bases of the Zionist resettlement
movements.[57]

---

[50] Halevy Numbers 84, 85.
[51] Halevy Number 94.
[52] Halevy Number 94b.
[53] Halevy Number 96.
[54] Halevy Number 117. Rosenheim, *op. cit.,* pp. 104-105, gave further details
concerning a large donation to the *Netzah Yisrael* schools mentioned in this letter.
[55] Among the Halevy papers (Number 158) was a record of pupils in the
Netzah Yisrael schools in 5672 (1912), in Halevy's handwriting: Petah Tikvah,
220; Rishon LeZion, 50; Ekron, 25; Rehovot, 25; Haifa, 50; and the Girls' School
in Petah Tikvah 88.
[56] Halevy Number 143a.
[57] Rosenheim, *op. cit.,* p. 96.

CHAPTER NINE

Architect of Agudath Israel

I T WAS ONLY A YEAR after Halevy had become affiliated with the *Freie Vereinigung* that he[1] projected the idea that the work of its Palestine Commission called for wider sponsorship. He was convinced that the time had come for launching an international Orthodox organization which would embrace all matters relating to the Holy Land including settlement projects. It was Halevy who suggested that this new movement be named Agudath Israel. While R. Salomon Breuer, the president of the *Freie Vereinigung,* was agreeable, it took much persuasion on Halevy's part to convince Jacob Rosenheim, its executive vice-president, of the merit of this undertaking. In one of his many letters to Rosenheim on the subject, Halevy observed that the *Freie Vereinigung* was limited in scope and did not have the forces needed for revitalizing Orthodoxy as would a world-wide movement of religious Jews.[2] Halevy felt that Rosenheim himself was also meant for greater heights.

At the beginning of the twentieth century another development taking place in Russia helped set the stage for the Agudah idea. Efforts at uniting Russian Orthodox Jewry were making headway under the guidance of such personalities as R. Israel Meir Kagan of Radun (the *Hafetz Haim*) and R. Haim Ozer Grodzensky of Vilna. Under the leadership of the Hassidic Rabbis of Gur and Czortkov a *rapprochement* had also begun within the strongholds of *hassidism.* Thus, in 1907, R. Grodzensky contemplated the

---

[1] Halevy Number 85.
[2] Halevy Number 86.

launching of an Orthodox newspaper for Russian Jewry. In response to R. Grodzensky's request for guidance in this matter, Halevy was ready with some practical advice. He pointed out[3] that at the start a weekly would be more realistic; a daily newspaper might prove to be too burdensome to maintain without the concomitant experience of the publishing phase, circulation expansion, and financial backing.

It should be noted that in the summer of 1903 a Congress of Orthodox Rabbis was convened in Cracow with representatives from many lands upon the initiative of the Rabbi of Cairo.[4] The official proceedings of this convocation, which was limited to rabbis, were published the same year.[5] While Halevy did not participate in this event, he was involved with the planning of another rabbinical conference in 1906.[6] Halevy had already been in the forefront of large scale meetings and undertakings dating back to his Vilna and Volozhin days.

As Halevy was finding his way in the organizational channels of the *Freie Vereinigung,* the path was opening for the leaders of the Jewries of greater Russia to come together with the initiators of the Agudah movement in Germany. In the light of Halevy's background and personality, the full significance of his role in the erection of the bridge between Russian Jewry and German Jewry which ultimately reached all the major Jewish communities throughout the world, can be readily appreciated. Halevy's wholehearted involvement with the Agudah idea was a decisive factor in allaying the fear of the rabbis of Eastern Europe. They were concerned that the union with organized Jewry in Western Europe would lead to a penetration of the German secular culture into their religiously-guarded circles.

[3] Halevy Number 46.
[4] *Hamelitz,* 25 Tamuz 5663, p. 1, *et seq.*
[5] "Protocol" in *Hapeles,* 5663.
[6] Halevy Number 26.

Were it not for the fact that Halevy was highly regarded by the luminaries of the rabbinical circles of Russia as well as by the Orthodox leadership of Germany, the idea of an organized rabbinically-oriented world religious organization at that time would not have been realized.

As for the Mizrachi which was founded in 1902 "as a religious party, though a distinct and separate faction within the Zionist movement,"[7] it was not in the good graces of many leading rabbis of Russia, Germany and Hungary because of its political Zionist affiliation.[8] The Mizrachi movement, nonetheless, had a following in Eastern Europe.

Halevy's thoughts on Zionism and the Mizrachi were distinctly recorded in two letters[9] which he wrote in 1904 (the year Herzl died), in response to queries[10] from the Chief Rabbi of Vienna, Moritz Guedemann,[11] and R. Joseph Samuel Bloch of Vienna.

In his letter to the former, Halevy referred to the critical reactions of the *Hatam Sofer* and R. Israel Salanter to R. Zvi Kalisher's *Dreeshat Zion*. He likewise took to task R. Samuel J. Rabinowitz's *Hadat Vehaleumiut* and R. Isaac J. Reines's *Or Hadash Al Zion*. Halevy was disturbed that Reines agreed with Nordau, an avowed antireligionist, in attacking those rabbis who avoided the Zionist movement. He further analyzed the non-religious elements in the nationalism of Herzl's ideology. His displeasure with the Mitzrachi stemmed from its political Zionist orientation. Thus he turned down an invitation to its conference called in Pressburg in 1904. He also took issue with Reines who

[7] Solomon Kerstein, "Mizrachi." *Universal Jewish Encyclopedia*, VII, p. 599.
[8] Rosenheim, *op. cit.*, p. 120.
[9] M. C. E. Bloch, *Mee Nattan Limesheesah Yaakov Veyisrael Levozezim*, pp. 163-172.
[10] *Ibid., pp.* 14, 52.
[11] He was the first man of standing whom Herzl took into his confidence, but he later rejected the new concept of nationalistic Judaism in his *Nationaljudentum*.

claimed in his book that one hundred and fifty rabbis subscribed to Zionism when in fact they went on record only in support of settlement in the Holy Land and such matters as the purchasing of its *etrogim*. In his letter to Bloch, Halevy concluded that he likewise endorsed with all his heart and soul the "colonization" work in the Holy Land.

A historian[12] far from the Agudah camp echoed Halevy's views when he noted that "the Agudists were, of course, dissatisfied with the religious, or areligious, attitude of official Zionism, but *Yishub Eretz Yisrael* (Resettlement of Palestine) stood forth as a biblical command and found the warmest support among the leading Agudist rabbis."

No wonder then that Halevy, who gave serious thought to the Orthodox approach to Judaism and Zionism, arrived at a solution, crystallized through his dedicated work in the *Freie Vereinigung*, which was culminated in the Agudah movement.

A report of a conference of the Palestine Commission of the *Freie Vereinigung* held on December 28, 1908 reflected the increasingly significant relationship of the *Vereinigung* toward the Holy Land out of which clearly emerged the idea of the Agudath Israel.[13] Ironically, Halevy had hesitated[14] to attend this meeting because of his financial circumstances. It was only after Rosenheim had written several letters asking him to come and had arranged to defray his traveling expenses that Halevy made the trip to Frankfurt. In a letter to his son, Samuel,[15] from the conference site, Halevy could not hold back his ebullience over the results of the proceedings. For it was then that Halevy was appointed to arrange the organizational meeting of the Agudah

12 I. Elbogen, *op. cit.,* p. 539.
13 *Die Freie Vereinigung, op. cit., p.* 11.
14 Halevy Number 87.
15 Halevy Number 88.

movement and to invite the outstanding rabbis of Russia to participate.[16]

Some nine months prior to the December conference Halevy had already worked on plans for the formation of the Agudah movement in Russia. In a letter to R. Haim Ozer Grodzensky,[17] a leader of the Russian rabbinate, Halevy was pleased to note that the Agudah idea was gaining popularity in Russia and that he had received encouraging responses from all corners of the land. He proposed that committees be organized without delay in all the large Jewish communities such as Vilna, Pinsk, Grodno, Riga, Vitepsk, and Moholev, so that the movement would assume a united structure. In cities where there were no capable leaders, it was vital to send qualified representatives to form such committees. Russian Jews, Halevy observed, were by nature impressed by deeds. Thus a dynamic movement led by the religious leaders and offering a practical program to counteract the prevalent negative forces in Jewish life, would attract the "whole house of Israel." He cited the ascendancy of the religious forces in Bad Homburg which would not have been possible without the successful reorganization of the *Freie Vereinigung* in Germany. The tragedy of Orthodoxy in Russia at the time, Halevy pointed out, was that although the religious elements were the electors, it was the freethinkers who held the reins in communal affairs and, while the religious elements were the readers, the writers were the freethinkers. Halevy wanted to see a cluster of religiously oriented writers replace the thirty or forty writers who made up the current popular Hebrew press.

Halevy was fully aware that the resuscitation of the Orthodoxy he envisioned would take some time. The very popularization of this goal, he was convinced, could have a salutary effect upon

16 Halevy Number 98; Rosenheim, *op. cit.*, p. 116.
17 Halevy Number 70.

religious circles since the realization of a problem is more than half the solution.

Halevy was also in contact with the Rabbi of Gur relating to these matters in the fall of 1907.[18]

The conference of the *Freie Vereinigung* with the "rabbis of Russia" was originally planned to take place in Koenigsberg after the *Shevuot* festival in 1909.[19] However, since the Russian Government had permitted a rabbinical conference to take place in Vilna on the thirteenth of Iyar, another one close to this date would not have been allowed, even if it were to be held in Germany. Accordingly, Halevy suggested that it be scheduled on *Shabbat Nahamu* in Bad Homburg, near Frankfurt. Halevy had also planned to attend that Vilna convocation in Iyar, but he could not make it.[20]

As has already been noted, Halevy knew personally most of the prominent rabbis in Russia from his Vilna and Volozhin days. Thus when Rosenheim informed Halevy that he was having difficulties in his negotiations with R. Haim Soloveichik, Halevy assured him[21] that he would win him over since they were "like brothers" as far back as their Volozhin days (in the 1880's).

While Rosenheim in his memoirs[22] acknowledged Halevy's key role in bringing together the East and West, his article in the *Universal Jewish Encyclopedia*[23] on the Agudath Israel did not mention Halevy's role when noting that during the years 1908-10 the *Freie Vereinigung* was advancing a plan for the formation of a world organization of traditional Jews.

Another testimony to Halevy's role in arranging this conference

[18] Halevy Number 54.
[19] Halevy Number 102.
[20] Halevy Number 103.
[21] Halevy Number 96.
[22] *Op. cit.*, pp. 115-116.
[23] Vol. I, p. 128.

was its taking place in the very quarters of his bosom friend, Heimann Kottek, the Rabbi of Bad Homburg, which was also his summer residence.

This gathering must have been regarded at the time as having historical significance since the Hebrew encyclopedia, *Ozar Yisrael*,[24] appearing shortly thereafter, already made mention of it as a "conclave of rabbis."

Halevy did not stand on ceremony with such personalities as R. Haim Ozer Grodzensky and others whom he had known from his younger days. It was in his contacts with those rabbis whom he did not know personally that his role as master strategist and diplomat came to the fore.

Halevy's letter to R. Shalom D. Schneersohn of Liubavich,[25] in which he invited him to the conference, revealed his approach to the rabbinical luminaries; it was carefully planned step by step. First Halevy arranged for Rosenheim to discuss this convocation with R. Schneersohn. Having received a favorable report, Halevy was ready to invite him formally, at which time he also gave him a compelling explanation of its purpose and timing. He mentioned too that R. Grodzensky had agreed to attend. Halevy did not hesitate to send him a follow-up letter[26] when no answer was forthcoming to his original invitation.

It was Halevy's expressed wish that there should be no advance publicity concerning his plans in order that the conference would not be undermined by any inimical forces. Thus *Der Israelit,* which was published by Rosenheim, made no mention of it beforehand. Halevy's concern about all aspects of this undertaking was typical of his sense of responsibility.

24 Vol. IV (New York, 1910), p. 118.
25 Halevy Number 98.
26 Halevy Number 101.

His invitation to R. Eliezer Gordon of Telshe[27] was sent later than the others because Halevy was at first under the impression that he was not up to traveling. Having learned of a pending trip of his, Halevy urged him to schedule it so that he would also be able to attend the conference in Bad Homburg. By then he was able to inform him that the Rabbi of Liubavich had agreed to come. As for the Rabbi of Gur, Halevy had arranged for R. Soloveichik to invite him personally.

Because of the forthcoming conference to launch the Agudah movement, Halevy considered the *Freie Vereinigung's* plans to send a delegation to the Holy Land in the spring of 1909 premature.[29] A circular had already gone off the press which mentioned Halevy's name among those who would be making this pilgrimage. However, the project did not materialize.

The Halevy correspondence revealed that Rosenheim depended upon Halevy's guidance as the date of the conference in Bad Homburg was drawing near. Difficult problems were continuously brought to his attention and solutions would always be forthcoming without delay. Rosenheim's descriptions in his autobiography of the events of those days have been further elucidated by Halevy's dynamic role which has come to light in part through his correspondence.

Since R. Salomon Breuer, who was president of the *Freie Vereinigung,* played a very important role in the proceedings which led to the Bad Homburg Conference, the problem of R. Marcus Horovitz's relationship to this conference was one that troubled Rosenheim.

Horovitz was a founder and vice-president of the *Deutscher Rabbinervarband* (General Union of German Rabbis) which

---

[27] Halevy Number 104.
[28] Halevy Number 98.
[29] Halevy Number 99.

included Reform and Orthodox rabbis. While there existed a traditional rabbinical organization, Breuer established the Orthodox Union of Rabbis which excluded rabbis who were members of the *Rabbinervarband*. Horovitz's *kehillah*, too, had a religiously controversial background. By the middle of the nineteenth century the old Frankfurt *kehillah* was taken over by the reformers. Through a bill passed in the German Parliament in 1876, Samson Raphael Hirsch achieved independence from the Reform congregation for his *kehillah*. The Reform congregation, fearful of an exodus of its Orthodox members, continued to maintain its Orthodox institutions on condition that the Orthodox element would retain their membership. Horovitz was the Rabbi of the *kehillah* of the Orthodox part of the Reform congregation, which was ostracized by both Hirsch and Breuer. It was evident that Horovitz could not be granted a leading role in the Agudath Israel.

In a letter[30] written two months before the conference, Halevy assured Rosenheim that there was no need for concern. He had planned to have R. Soloveichik and R. Schneersohn meet with Horovitz following the conference, to pacify him. Halevy was on very good terms with Horovitz who was instrumental in publishing the first volume of the *Dorot Harishonim* and had a hand in Halevy's appointment as *Klausrabbiner* in Hamburg. Nonetheless he felt that Horovitz's ideology was not in harmony with the program of the Agudah. Halevy observed that Horovitz and his circle considered religious Jewry as a minority which was entitled to the same personal rights within the Jewish community as any other minority. In contrast, Halevy posited the Agudah ideology that Torah-observing Jews constitute fundamental Jewry, no matter what their number, as cited in

---

30 Halevy Number 105.

the *Zohar*,[31] "God, Torah and Israel are one." Thus the formal organization of all Orthodox Jews would be the contemporary projection of the dictum in the *Zohar*.

In describing his aspirations to R. Schneersohn,[32] Halevy had in mind an all-embracing Orthodox organization with status to be in a position to counteract the growing secular influences of the *Alliance Israelite Universelle* and the *Hilfsverein der Deutschen Juden* on the world scene as well as in the Holy Land. He pointed out that while an organization of international scope would not be tolerated in Russia by the Czarist government, it could thrive in Germany where there would be no interference and would at the same time be centrally located.

Among the distinguished personalities attending the Bad Homburg Conference were the Rabbis Haim Soloveichik, Abraham M. Alter of Gur, Haim Ozer Grodzensky of Vilna, Eliezer Gordon of Telshe, Eliezer Rabinowitz of Minsk, representatives of Shalom Duber Schneersohn of Liubavich and David Friedman of Karlin, as well as the leading laymen from St. Petersburg, Warsaw, Lodz, Riga, and the president of the Federation of the Religious Communities of Hungary, Adolf Frankel.

The Bad Homburg Conference was confronted with parochial viewpoints that were not in consonance with Halevy's views. Breuer[33] and the Hungarian delegation wanted to project their *austritt* ideology into the program and thereby rule out from membership in the Agudah all those who belonged to mixed (Orthodox and non-Orthodox) Jewish communal and political

---

[31] *Aharei*, 73.

[32] Halevy Number 98.

[33] His opposition to the more liberal tendencies in the Agudah was well known as noted in the *Universal Jewish Encyclopedia*, II, p. 525, and *Jewish Chronicle*, London, Aug. 9, 1912, p. 11.

bodies.[34] The public relations problem in regard to the Holy Land projects also became entangled in differences of opinion. Considering the many problems and the noncompromising attitudes of the participants at the Bad Homburg Conference, it is evident that were it not for Halevy's sustaining efforts behind the scenes, the Agudah idea would have dissipated right then and there.

Following the Bad Homburg Conference, which lasted over two weeks, the activities of the Planning Committee gradually slowed down to a virtual standstill. The internal situation in Russia also hindered communication among its rabbis on the subject. Halevy's correspondence, however, revealed that his activities did not slacken in furthering the Agudah program. Nor did he neglect his leading role in the Palestine Commission of the *Freie Vereinigung.*

In a letter to Rosenheim[35] not long after the Conference, Halevy alluded to his formulation of a constitution for the Agudah. Among the Halevy papers was such a draft[36] in his own handwriting to accompany this letter. Under Article I, entitled, "Name of Organization and Its Headquarters," was the brief statement, "The scattered of Israel in all places unite to form a society by the name, 'Agudath Israel,' to strengthen Judaism, with headquarters in Frankfurt a.m." Article II was entitled, "Purposes of the Agudah." It listed four points: 1) United action for Torah observance and representation; 2) Furtherance of Torah educational institutions, especially in the Holy Land and the new communities in America and Africa; 3) Improvement of the economic as well as spiritual levels of Jews; 4) Popularization

---

34 Rosenheim, *op. cit.,* pp. 120-124.

35 Halevy Number 110.

36 Halevy Number 110a.

of Jewish literature through scholarly personalities and the publication of newspapers with meaningful content in consonance with the Jewish heritage.

Halevy's role in the preparation of the "statutes" of the Agudah was well known within the Agudah circles.[37]

Inasmuch as Halevy was abreast of the intellectual spirit of the times, he strongly emphasized the importance of scholarship within the framework of the Agudah as a vital element in elevating the prestige of the movement.

Toward the end of 1909 plans were under way to have R. Yehiel Mihel Ascher of Neuchatel, Switzerland, travel on behalf of the Agudah movement to Russia, England and America. Halevy[38] thought it best that Ascher visit England and America first. He also insisted that this project remain a secret until it would have been carried out. It was practical thinking on his part not to divulge plans of a public nature until they were realized, thereby avoiding many potentially embarrassing situations. As a matter of fact Ascher never did reach America.

An unexpected impetus was given to the organizational structure of the Agudah in the wake of the tenth Zionist Congress in Basel in the summer of 1911. At that *Kultur-Kongress* it was resolved that the combination of Zionism and Jewish nationalism was the *raison d'etre* for the twentieth-century Jew. Accordingly the Zionists planned to establish a system of national Jewish education devoid of religion. Although the Mizrachists were acquiescent in Zionist political and economic matters, they refused to go along with the Zionists on such a fundamental matter as education; in the formative years of childhood there could be no indifference where religion is concerned. The Mizrachi Federation's struggle against the Zionists' educational policy, however, was fruitless. In the aftermath of the Mizrachi's defeat,

[37] E. A. Rabinowitz in *Hamodia,* 26 Iyar 5674, p. 468.
[38] Halevy Number 112.

an emergency conference of the Mizrachi was held in Berlin in September.[39] Twelve of the thirty-five Mizrachi delegates present withdrew from the Zionist Organization. Concomitantly, a stirring article in *Der Israelit*[40] entitled, "The Needs of the Day," by the Rabbi of Basel, Arthur Cohn, called upon the faithful adherents of the Torah to unite in forming an independent world organization. Some of the leaders of the Frankfurt Mizrachi, who also were delegates at the Zionist Congress, enthusiastically joined the *Freie Vereinigung* circle in forming the Provisional Committee for the Founding of the Agudath Israel. This group was entrusted with planning its first formal meeting.

Thus it came about that a special gathering of fifty-five[41] representatives of Orthodox Jewry from many lands assembled in Frankfurt, in October 1911, at which a resolution was passed to establish the Agudath Israel Organization. It was decided to convene in Kattowitz for the organizational conference in 1912. Halevy was appointed to the Provisional Committee. Many unsolved problems remained in the wake of this conference—some old, some new.[42]

While this meeting was successful in terms of its main goals, serious opposition suddenly erupted from the German rabbis, including Breuer, because the rabbinate had not been represented there.[43] Halevy had to explain that this gathering was primarily concerned with the financial structure and not with fundamental matters. He alluded to the fact that these hindrances based on pettiness were affecting his health. He pleaded with his friend,

[39] J. L. Fishman, *Sefer Hamizrahi*, p. 272; H. Schwab, *History of Orthodox Jewry in Germany*, p. 116.

[40] Aug. 31, 1911, p. 1.

[41] Halevy Number 141. According to Rosenheim, *op. cit.*, p. 123, there were 47 delegates.

[42] Rosenheim, *ibid.*, pp. 125-137, recorded many details of this gathering, including resumes of many of the speeches.

[43] Halevy Number 141.

Kottek, to use his influence with those rabbis not to oppose the development of the movement, whose failure would be as tragic as the destruction of the *Bet Hamikdash*. He was fearful of the repercussions to the *Freie Vereinigung* as well as to Orthodoxy in general if all the efforts in creating the Agudah idea would be thwarted. For a time there was also some doubt as to whether or not the Hungarian delegation would attend the forthcoming Kattowitz Conference.[44]

Halevy's sense of organizational responsibility was unusual for one who was primarily a scholarly person. Prior to the Kattowitz Conference he wrote to Rosenheim[45] that it was vital for the Agudah to have a dynamic paid staff and "bureau" in order for it to expand as a world organization. He felt that the expense of a well organized headquarters would not only pay for itself in a short time, but that it would make the difference between a vibrant movement and a contained effort. It was at this time that Halevy began to impress Rosenheim with the thought that he was destined for even more eminent posts than those of publisher of *Der Israelit* and administrator of the *Freie Vereinigung*. The idea of having Rosenheim ultimately assume the leadership of Agudath Israel was likewise Halevy's. In a subsequent letter to Rosenheim[46] a year after the Kattowitz Conference, Halevy pictured the type of an Agudah representative from Germany that would appeal to Russian Jewry. It was evident that Rosenheim matched the description.

The town of Kattowitz, located on the upper Silesian border between Germany and Austria, had already become a historic name in modern Jewish life. It was there that the first conference of the *Hovevei Zion* was held. In some quarters it was felt that

---

[44] Halevy Number 159.
[45] Halevy Number 142a.
[46] Halevy Number 159.

just as the first conference in Kattowitz spearheaded the Zionist movement, so would this "second Kattowitz" lead to a successful world religious movement. Meir Berlin[47] (Bar-Ilan), a renowned Mizrachi leader noted at the time that if a strong international Orthodox organization would be established, the Zionists would have to recognize it and respect its decisions based on religious principles. Many circles primarily concerned with religious matters on the local scene were now convinced that an Agudath Israel was a necessity. The Mizrachi periodical, *Haivri*,[48] reported that many of its executive members were planning to attend the conclave.

Of interest was the favorable publicity by the Jewish press on the eve of the Conference. The remarks in the *Jewish Chronicle*[49] were particularly encouraging: "Whatever be one's attitude towards the principles of Orthodox Judaism, it cannot be denied that as far as numbers go, the Orthodox form the largest and strongest party in Judaism and that hitherto it has not been organized. The other tendencies in Judaism gathered their strength from the Orthodox ranks. It is incontestable, therefore, that a union among Orthodox Jews signifies at the same time the strengthening of the Jewish people; hence tomorrow will be regarded as a landmark in the history of the Jewish people if it brings us what our leaders expect of it: an organization of Orthodox Judaism . . . It is to be hoped that this conference will have the desired result, not alone because the most important Rabbis of Russia are strongly in favour of the movement; not alone because all the German Rabbis hold but one view with regard to the Agudas Yisroel, however differently they may think on other matters; but chiefly because the recognized leaders of

---

[47] *Fun Volozhin Biz Yerushalayim*, pp. 430-433.
[48] 8 Sivan 5672, p. 205.
[49] London, May 31, 1912, p. 11.

Orthodox thought and the best known Jewish scholars in Germany are among those who have summoned the Conference. They are Dr. David Hoffmann, Rector of the Rabbinical Seminary in Berlin, whose disciples are the most Orthodox Rabbis in Germany; the renowned historian, Isak Halevy, of Hamburg, author of *Doroth Harischonim;* Dr. Jacob Feuchtwanger, founder and late President of the Misrachi Federation; and many others."

The Kattowitz Conference was called for May 27 and 28, 1912. Halevy's name was among the four German members of the temporary Rabbinical Council who signed the formal invitations to a limited number of distinguished personalities (the others were Breuer, Wolf Feilchenfeld and Hoffmann). Inasmuch as Halevy did not seek any publicity in such matters one may surmise that he was a signatory because his name would be of special significance to the rabbis of the Russian domains.

Among the many rabbinical luminaries who sent their apologies that they were unable to attend the Conference were Abraham I. Kook of Safed and Bernard Revel of Philadelphia.[50]

As for Halevy's role in Kattowitz, no published record has revealed the entire story.[51] But in a letter to his close friend, Kottek,[52] Halevy noted that he was unable to communicate with him in the pre-Kattowitz days because he was occupied with the preparations to the point of exhaustion; and during the Conference he was occupied endlessly behind the scenes in conciliating R. Soloveichik on one side and R. Breuer on the other, as well as with keeping a finger on the pulse of all the proceedings.

[50] *Mikhtevay Brakhah Vehaskamah Me'ayt Gedolei Doreinu Shelo Hispeeku Lavo El Ha'asayfah BeKattovitz,* Frankfurt, 5673.

[51] Halevy's name is conspicuously missing in Adolf Weyl's article describing the founding of the Agudah, *"Die Vorgeschichte der 'Agudas Jisroel,'"* in the documentary, *Agudas Jisroel Berichte und Materialien herausgegeben vom Provisorischen Comite de 'Agudas Jisroel' zu Frankfurt a.m.*

[52] Halevy Number 150.

While Meir Berlin[53] credited Halevy with mediating the views of the East and the West at the Conference, his conjectures of Halevy's motives indicated that he was not aware of Halevy's selfless efforts.

It was after the Conference got under way that Meir Berlin wrote in the *Haivri*[54] that Zionism should really be but one aspect of Jewish life and that the Agudath Israel ideology represents the historic concept of *klal Yisrael* (the people of Israel) based on the holy Torah. A full report of the Conference also found its way into the *Haivri*[55] (Berlin was its editor). Having attended the Conference, Berlin was deeply impressed with the idealistic spirit and goals set forth there. It is interesting to note that he had written to Rosenheim expressing the desire to be appointed to the secretarial position of the Agudath Israel.[56]

Berlin's remarks in his autobiography concerning R. Soloveichik's relationship with the Agudah are also subject to revision in light of the Halevy correspondence. Contrary to Berlin's impressions, R. Soloveichik's participation in both the Bad Homburg and Kattowitz Conferences was not limited merely to his presence there. Many letters were exchanged between him and Halevy relating to the Agudah from the days of the Bad Homburg Conference. R. Soloveichik caused a stir at the Kattowitz Conference by his presentation of "eighteen points" which were his conditions in order to remain in the Agudah and also by his signing an *issur* upon the request of R. Breuer, which he later rescinded.[57] Halevy continued his negotiations with R. Soloveichik concerning his "eighteen points" even after the Conference ended.[58]

---

[53] *Fun Volozhin Biz Yerushalayim,* pp. 430-437.
[54] May 31, 1912, p. 213.
[55] June 14, 1912, pp. 225-230.
[56] Rosenheim, *op. cit.,* p. 186.
[57] *Ibid.,* pp. 184-185.
[58] Halevy Number 157.

Berlin[59] omitted an important fact when he noted that R. Soloveichik's interest in the Agudah gradually waned after the Kattowitz Conference — his apathy was due to Halevy's death in 1914. Having been "as brothers" since their youth, R. Soloveichik's interest in the Agudah was nurtured by Halevy. Halevy's absence from the scene was evidently a major factor in his not becoming involved with new contacts at this stage in his life; politics was not his forte.

At the Conference it was decided to elect a *Vaad Rabbanim* (Rabbinical Council) to be composed of world renowned Talmudic scholars. Among those elected, with R. Soloveichik on the top of the list, was Halevy. Yet a year later Halevy[60] expressed his strong disapproval of Breur's suggestion to name this body, *Vaad Gedolei Harabbanim* (Council of Great Rabbis).

Even with unanimity of purpose at the Kattowitz Conference, Rosenheim returned home from the proceedings with a heavy heart. It was pitiful that the ideals of the organizers of this unique gathering were diluted in some measure by the differences among the heterogeneous views.[61] Rosenheim[62] in his memoirs summed up those trying days with a tribute to Halevy who stood at his side with moral support and outstanding wisdom. He referred to Halevy as his guiding light in laying the foundations of the Agudah.

In the post-Kattowitz days Halevy continued his intense activities embracing all aspects of the Agudah organization. Among the Halevy papers was a letter from Mordecai Rabinowitz of Skidel (Russia),[63] to R. Jacob Lipschitz of Kovno, who was active

[59] *Op. cit.,* p. 437.
[60] Halevy Number 156.
[61] Rosenheim, *op. cit.,* pp. 187-198, and Schwab, *op. cit.,* pp. 117-120, related the major areas of contention.
[62] *Ibid.,* p. 198.
[63] Dated 20 Heshvan, 5674.

in Agudah circles, in which he acknowledged receiving an invitation to become general secretary of the Agudath Israel at its headquarters in Frankfurt. He assured Lipschitz that he would inform Halevy of his decision. Halevy[64] was also preoccupied with counteracting false rumors that were being spread about the Agudah.

Halevy was in the forefront of propagandizing the Agudah among the Russian rabbinate.[65] He was ready to receive criticism concerning the Agudah which could be utilized to improve the movement in the course of its development. He also sensed that the time was ripe for sending an Agudah organizational representative to the United States.[66]

Halevy's wholehearted devotion and dedication to the Agudah was clearly evidenced in his response to Rosenheim[67] when he was asked to perform some task that was disagreeable to him; he remarked that he was prepared to bear any burden on behalf of the Agudath Israel.

Two events of critical impact on the Agudah movement occurred in 1914. First (chronologically) was the passing of Halevy on May 15 (20 Iyar, 5674). The second was the outbreak of World War I, which disrupted Jewish communal life on the entire Continent.

The subsequent course of events confirmed[68] that more than poetic language was spoken when Halevy was eulogized as the soul of the Agudath Israel. Halevy's sudden departure from the Agudah scene in its formative years was indeed a misfortune that this movement could ill afford. For a time the movement seemed to have lost much of its impetus. Following the war, however,

---

64 Halevy Number 160.
65 Halevy Numbers 157, 161.
66 Halevy Number 160.
67 *Idem.*
68 Rosenheim, *op. cit.,* pp. 208ff.; Schwab, *op. cit.,* pp. 121ff.

the tempo was regained and the Agudah attracted an impressive following throughout the world.

Halevy's primary concern in launching this movement was the same as in his polemical writings on Jewish history — to bring into proper focus the eternal element of our holy *mesorah* (heritage) and to infuse into the modern Orthodox scene a dynamic, creative spirit. Halevy's selfless dedication to this cause has deeply influenced Jewish life. His ideas have endured as a moving force in the development of the Agudah approach to Jewish needs and aspirations.

CHAPTER TEN

Epilogue

I T WAS SIX YEARS after Halevy experienced the financial debacle which compelled him to leave his home and to wander from country to country that he began to emerge as a major Jewish historian and leading figure in the *Juedisch-Literarische Gesellschaft*, the *Freie Vereinigung*, and the Agudath Israel. Even in his portentous misfortunes and poverty, Halevy was always in the vanguard as the defender of his people's spiritual heritage, on both the intellectual and communal battlefronts. His enduring accomplishments as well as his inner thoughts as revealed in the correspondence bore witness that his distressing experiences did not dampen his idealism nor blur his spiritual *Weltanschauung*.

Halevy's public career starting from his early Vilna days was marked by his consistent avoidance of personal publicity. It has been very difficult to trace his many cogent articles in the *Halevanon* and *Hamelitz* which were unsigned. Nor was it generally known that the Volozhin Yeshiva was dependent in a large measure on Halevy's efforts. He played his vital role in the launching and development of the Agudah movement behind the scenes. Thus his name did not appear among the speakers at the Bad Homburg and Kattowitz Conferences, the birth places of the Agudah, as well as at any other public gatherings. In a letter[1] relating to his efforts for the Agudath Israel, Halevy noted that he bent backwards to keep his name out of the limelight. His personality was geared to deeds rather than to public fanfare.

---

[1] Halevy Number 161.

Halevy's self imposed social isolation stemmed in part from his concern that he would not be properly understood. Thus he urged[2] his friend, Kottek, to join him at an important conference of the *Freie Vereinigung* because he was apprehensive that he would not find himself comfortable there. He likewise confided to Kottek that he decided against attending a wedding out-of-town because he considered his presence there would not be in keeping with the dignity of the Torah.[3]

Halevy's strong determination to carry out his obligations was evident in the course of his activities within the *Freie Vereinigung* and the Agudah. It was in this spirit that he wrote to Rosenheim[4] that when the welfare of his people was involved he was ready to endure excessive hardships.

Halevy had his share of bitter enemies. That did not deter him from utilizing them through intermediaries in his concern for others.[5]

The Halevy correspondence reflected Halevy's evaluations of the addressees in the salutations. Thus R. Haim Soloveichik was the only one who was given the elevated title, *Hagaon Ha'amiti Hamefursam Pe'er Hador*. His signature, however, was uniform in all his correspondence after he left Russia, "Yitzhak Isaac Halevy."

The rare smile-producing lines in the Halevy correspondence were written in a tone of sarcasm: one described a comedy of errors[6] and another made a caustic reference to a physician whose mastery of *hokhmat Yisrael* was equated by Halevy to his own knowledge of medical science.[7]

---

[2] Halevy Numbers 60, 61.
[3] Halevy Number 34.
[4] Halevy Number 96.
[5] Halevy Number 111.
[6] Halevy Number 19.
[7] Halevy Number 90.

In 1905 Halevy was subjected to confining heart illnesses.[8] In the midst of his varied activities he wrote to Kottek on occasions that he was physically weak.[9]

Halevy's fame as *gaon* and scholar was based on self-discipline. His correspondence reveals that there is no short cut to scholarship. Halevy was punctilious with the time he designated for his concentrated studies,[10] especially during the winter months when there were times that his correspondence was relegated to the "hour that was neither day nor night." His work did not slacken even during his illness if he could help it.[11] Thus he managed to keep up with his historical research in the course of his dynamic communal activities. He arranged to postpone an important meeting of the *Freie Vereinigung* so that he could complete his work on a particular subject in which he was deeply engrossed.[12]

Halevy's consideration for the feelings of others, notwithstanding his reputation for being outspoken, is worthy of mention. He asked Kottek not to convey his displeasure regarding some articles that had been published in the *Jahrbuch* to its editor because it would not serve any purpose.[13] He spoke up for the historian, Jawitz, for financial aid although he had some misgivings about his views.[14] On an *erev Pesah* when Halevy had already written a letter to Rosenheim concerning some controversial matter, he had second thoughts about mailing it. Instead he penned a second one in which he informed Rosenheim that he could not send his original letter on the eve of the festival and that it would be dispatched several days later.[15]

8 Halevy Number 10.
9 Halevy Numbers 143, 148.
10 Halevy Numbers 35, 112, 130, 131, 139.
11 Halevy Numbers 99, 134, 148.
12 Halevy Number 124.
13 Halevy Number 79.
14 Halevy Number 66.
15 Halevy Number 156.

In explaining some of his actions to Kottek[16] Halevy confided that his preoccupation with the truth transcended even personal considerations. This trait led to his inordinate outspokenness in his works and in his correspondence.

In the face of his many despairing situations, Halevy's faith in the Almighty never faltered. During the periods of poverty and distress he exerted himself even more in the service of his Creator.

Just as he delved into *hokhmat Yisrael* to confirm the historic faith of the Jew, so did he penetrate the foundations of faith. He was convinced that faith was an integral aspect of every being; one who denies the Almighty turns to serving false gods with zeal.[17]

The opening entry in Halevy's first manuscript was the dictum of the *Talmud Yerushalmi*:[18] "This verse should not depart from you, 'God of hosts is with us; the God of Jacob is our stronghold.' "[19]

Halevy's observations on human nature in his correspondence are worthy of mention: "The realization of a matter is more than half the deed and it leads to immediate action"[20] and "It is a general rule that action leads to one's goal."[21] These thoughts reflected Halevy's own creative approach to his life's goals; in all his undertakings he had a positive and dynamic outlook. He made those about him aware of his trust in his causes and in his own self-confidence.

As for the Halevy family, only meager information could be gleaned from his correspondence and from some relatives.

---

[16] Halevy Number 123.

[17] S. Halevy, *op. cit.,* pp. 52-54.

[18] *Berakhot,* Chap. V, Halakha 1.

[19] Psalms XLVI:8. This verse is found thrice in the daily morning service: following the order of the incense, section following *Barukh Sheamar,* and in the *Uva LeZion.*

[20] Halevy Number 70.

[21] Halevy Number 134.

A sister of Halevy, who was orphaned at the age of three and was raised by her grandfather, married into a Rubinstein family of Poneviz. Her son, Dr. Leopold Rubinstein, resides in England.

Halevy's daughter, Faiga, became the wife of Raphael Poker of a well-to-do family in Jassy, Rumania.[22] Halevy stayed in their home for several years in the course of his travels after he had left Vilna for good in 1895 until he settled in Germany. Their two sons later spent some time at Halevy's home in Hamburg. The elder, Elias, was also with Halevy in Bad Homburg in 1910[23] and the younger, Moses, was with him in Bad Homburg two summers later.[24] The latter along with his sisters, Jehudit Klughaupt and Rahel Lesser, reside in Israel.

Another daughter of Halevy, Sarah Leah, married into the philanthropic Chavkin family of Riga, Latvia.[25] She had several children. For a time preceding World War II the Chavkins lived in Rumania. One daughter married a Persitz of Russian background and they settled in Paris.

A son of Halevy, Mordecai Eliezer, was a student at the Volozhin Yeshiva at the time of its closing.[26] Halevy expressed his concern for him in his autobiographical notes soon after his exodus from Vilna. In 1909, R. Haim Soloveichik mentioned Mordecai Eliezer in a letter[27] to Halevy, reassuring him of his son's well-being. Mordecai Eliezer did not marry and died at an early age.

Another son, Nahum Haim, settled in England, where he was engaged in business and adopted the surname Robbins. He married Rose Stiller in the Great Synagogue of London in 1903.

---

[22] Halevy Number 121.
[23] *Loc. cit.*
[24] Halevy Number 152.
[25] Halevy Number 99.
[26] S. Halevy, *op. cit.*, p. 28.
[27] *Ibid.*, p. 65.

Their two daughters, Mrs. Blanche Wiener and Mrs. Stella Hannah Leigh, reside in England. He died in 1952.

Halevy's close relationship with his son, Samuel, has already been recorded in this work in the chapter on the Literati.[28]

Halevy was actively engaged in his scholarly writings and in his Agudah contacts until he was struck by a heart attack in the course of his usual evening walk. Three weeks later, on Friday night, 20 Iyar 5674 (May 15, 1914), he died in a Hamburg hospital.

In accordance with Halevy's will the family requested that no eulogies be delivered at the funeral. Jacob Rosenheim spoke briefly in the chapel of the hospital where the funeral commenced on Sunday. An unusual honor was accorded Halevy when the entire assemblage accompanied the funeral procession on foot the whole way to the Langenfelde Cemetery. His study table was used in making his coffin.[29]

Memorial meetings were held in honor of Halevy's memory in many Jewish communities in the weeks following the funeral.

In Halevy's life we behold a giant of mind and action in both scholarship and piety. His selfless dedication to his spiritual heritage will be a fount of inspiration for generations to come.

---

[28] See above pp. 87-89.

[29] *Der Gemeindebote Beilage zur Allgemeine Zeitung des Judentums,* Berlin, May 29, 1914, p. 3; *Der Israelit,* May 21, 1914, p. 3.

Letters

Number 1 to Dr. Jehuda Loeb Kantor, 29 Iyar 5647

בה יום ה' ג' סיון תר"ס

לרעות כבוד ידיד נפשי ורבי הרב הגאון הגדול האפורים החריף

וכו' בכל חדרי תורה אוהד ורבני וכו' ... כ"ר הורויץ הגאב"ד

ק"ק פפד"מ יצ"ו

הרבה שלום חיים עד העולם

יקרת ... אתן תודה ... ... בני כבוד גאונו ש'

והרבה בברכת החג

ועל דבר הענין הגדול ... כי אין אנו רשאי לבטל בית האב

הדבר גדול כזה הנוגע לתלמוד תורה דרבים וכו' ... ... כי על כל פנים

... אחר ... ...

אמנם זה ... כי הדבר לבריך ... ... וכן ... ...

...

יחזקו את החם הזה שלנו ועל כל ישראל ... ...

ויתברכו ... ... כל ... טובה ... ...

...

וכתבו ... כנפש רוח ...

נאם אוהבו ...

Number 3 to Rabbi Marcus Horovitz, 3 Sivan 5660

Number 26a to Rabbi Heimann Kottek, 27 Tishrei 5667

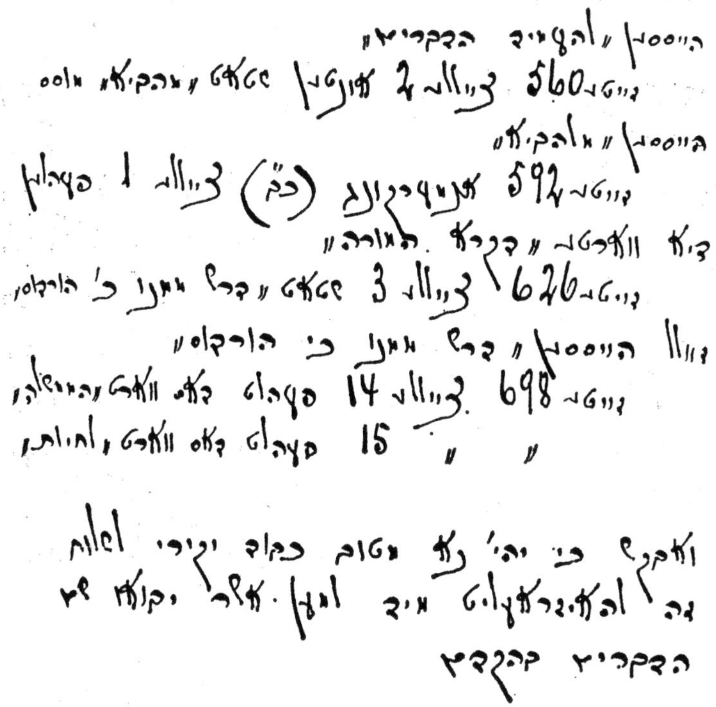

Number 26a Side Two

ב"ה יום ד' כ"ח תשרי

למעלת כבוד ידיד נפשי ולבבי הרב הג' המפורסם
הנכבד המפואר נגיד וחו"ב נעלה מוהר"ש שי' ד"ר
קאטטעק הגאבד"ק דק"ק האמבורג וכל אשר לו ברכה ושלום

תמול כתבתי במכתבי, ואחר זה קבלתי מכתב מידידי
הרב הגאון ר' חיים עוזר שי' מוויסבאדען ובסופו
מכתבו [struck-through word] ובקש לשלוח לו ספרי החדש ואמרה"י ויהי'
ו.י. ושענגעים והש"ב נפשי ועוד קימי לקחתי כה"ו ואפני
פי רצ"א. לבקרו אצל נפשי אבקש תי' מצוה בזאת
לה"ש נפשו ואז יהי' טוב לפני כבוד ידידי. לשלוח
אל.ו לוויסבאדען ספר מבורך ועל אשר יהי'
קירובו כבר נראות קלקלת הבאה, הוא הנהו מין
גדול, ולדעתי יהי' אפשר אחר זה לדבר עמו גם
בנוגע לדבר חקורתינו.
האדרעסע אל.ו על שמו

Rabbiner Ch. O. Grodsensky
in Wisbagen Beren str. N 3

אם לא שלח גאלדע ספרים מבורכים מחלק ראשון
כלו. רק מחלק ב' וחלק ג' שלח עשרה ספרים

Number 26b to Rabbi Heimann Kottek, 28 Tishrei 5667

Number 26b Side Two

Number 30 to Rabbi Heimann Kottek, 4 Tevet 5667

ומפורסמים פלאין

והנה טום יולם לקלות ען נב קעם אלבסקין

מ...ואלאתני רין דל דכרו ויורו אלא כתם בכר

ואלוים...נלא נב דפסים ואלוות הינה כ ין ןו וכי

נב אל אסמ הלרסיןל יסל קעורו ואלאר ליכר קורו

ואם נחנר את דל הכם כון יאון ואלאר הלוסיר

הלאות אלת דל דרכם קתנירה

ונ,ים רל ויורו ולורא אלרון את הבלולורסים

כרנסאת ההוא

ואם קיוטן ואליסאי אין יולה מלינון אדרים

הלרסי,רל ..את, אל אסור נב כה אאתר, ורבו

אלר,א ,נים ויורי אדוקיסאן דן ניאה

אראה לכ כהר הולאא הסמר רין קורסא

מאודלילכ ואסן לסוא סוונ אסמר הלן

כותם קתסברה, ואלנ יקיסל אאסבו ננרעל דרל

סוט , לאם לעווים ללוס

ישס

בה יום ה' כ"ג תשרי תרס"ח

לעולת כבוד ידידי הרב הג' המפורסים יקר ואציל ועוז
וכבוד י' ד' בלאזעצקער הגאלהר דֿק להנ' ברכה ושלום

יחד עם כל הנני אות חודה את הלנויי על החליפת
אמעצן כדלו. אך אסבר כי לא ה' לריך לסבור אתרא
מלוזן לאחד והבית נלנה בלגאות הנמולות, אפא מאעת
או בפרים ואתחון מלונה מעואות היותר אולכרתי
ונולר זה ההכרת להיר ליוד על הבפרים הלה
כמאור 7-6 וא הבקר עלהדיגינוט סעות
והוא אלי ובכיר לא ה' ואל מ' הגלא מן גאלוזאל מר
רהי כי לאי מן לאיד אחרי אלא ה' לא אונ נלוה לבוי
הוא לא מן רפי גאולאו אל פאך וא ארחוו כלא אחול
כי לאר לאחו יהודה אלה הוא ה' הבלוד והונכר פל
מורים אכן הול. והוא מלאות ה' הגלא אחרי מן גאלוזאל
ליבק לאחרי אות רפן גאולאל מר רמי ה' לא לרא
הגל ה' יהודה והוא ד' יהודה נלאה הרפין
והו יקורית על דבר הגלאיי הלא פלורית פל
כך עבמפל וחידושלוו פא כי לק חמבה הוא לאחו כי
מלואה קיסו. ו הרו וא כעל אלו אלל לדיגעום ומוד

הנקרים ... אל העיר על נה כל... הדבאל...
נקו. והנכיר ... כי אל אדלם ... ויבץ לציו...
כי הענשדם ה' הידי, כל כל ... נום והנכיר ...
כה.אד.הדמק

אול. כהד נכל נעות כחידו תכוק. עילקא
אדעיד ול...א... ... דהד ... כה.נהת יכ יכלק,
ולאל כי אל תנכל ותכלה ... קאמיו כי ל כהם
יכ כלנכס יאהל ... אהל כהל נה הקלתי מדקי
כי אל דול ותכלה ... ונה יה' אהנעות גהו
והחתה הלכהבה אך עלב נה כיהנל, וכהל ... יקים
א כי נעא הכל על לאו

קודלא, ... ל הדח ל ...
הוה כר האבאל ... ל

אדנ.. ... ... נום
ולהם לונעך ...

das dabei vorkommende Wort σαββατεις
giebt Epiphanius durch Synagoge
wieder, die Kleinasiatischen Juden
nannten also ihr Bethaus weil
sie es nur am Sabbat zu Besuchen
pflegen σαββατεις.

Number 60 to Rabbi Heimann Kottek, 3 Hanukkah 5668

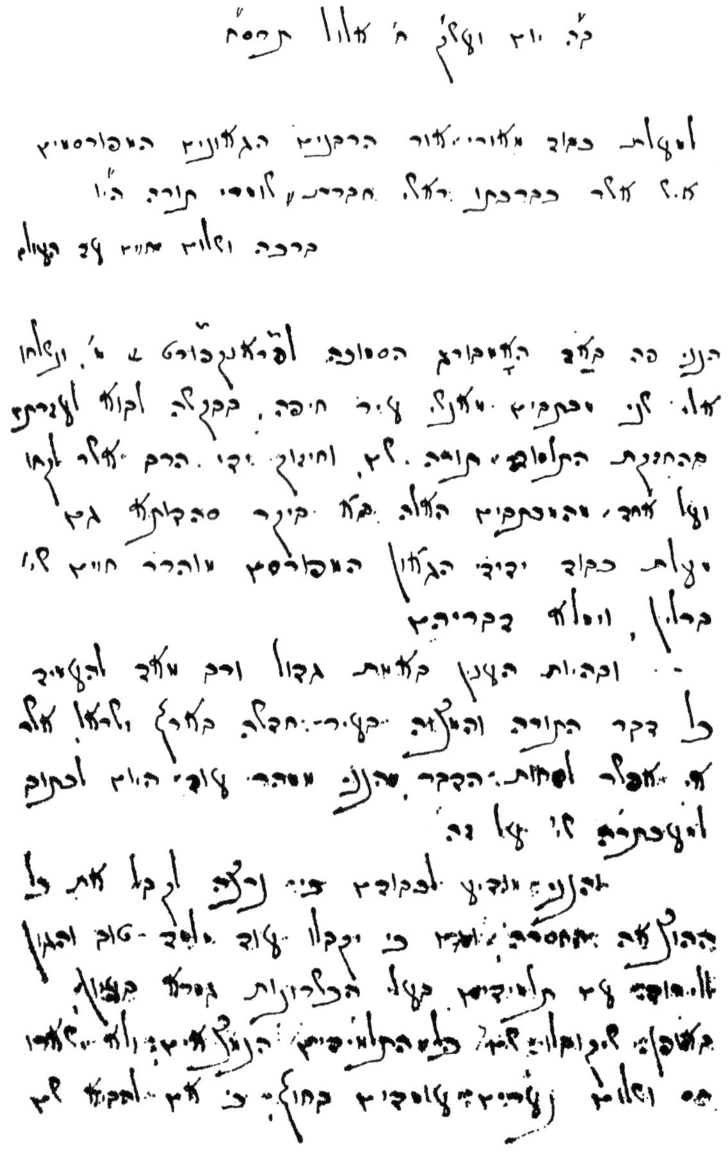

ב״ה יום ועש״ק ח׳ אלול תרס״ח

לשלום כבוד אדוני מורי הרבנים הגאונים המפורסמים

[illegible] חברת שומרי תורה הי״ו

ברכה ושלום [illegible] עד העולם

Number 81 to Shomrei Torah Society, 8 Elul 5668

וחייים כול הוברי. וגם אחנק יכי הרכ י', כי יה' קיכו
היעוחה והוגייה יו הומוע חובכ כול הוברי, והוחרכו
. כול כמו ,וחנק יש וחת כו וויכי היהכות

והוב־יכו֟ נה הולּא יסוכ הכבר הגכאו וולר
הֹונ וُיתֹקבֹולﬞﬦ הׁﬤﬥ עﬦﬞ﬩ ,ולּראו ﬡﬨﬦ כול ולר כחר
הוהﬡﬣﬤ ﬦﬥﬨﬦﬡﬨ כחוﬣ﬩, וﬥﬨﬦ חﬤﬥﬨ הﬧﬨﬦ וﬡﬥﬨﬦﬨ נה
כול ולר־ חﬧﬦﬨ ﬩ﬤﬨﬦﬦ ﬧﬨﬦﬡ'

וﬡ﬩ﬧﬨﬨ חﬧﬦﬨ וﬡﬨﬦ ﬦ' חﬤﬤﬧ כﬦ ﬦﬡﬦ הﬦﬧﬦﬡﬧﬦﬦ
וﬤﬧﬦ הﬤﬦﬡﬦ ה﬩ﬦ ﬧﬦﬡﬦﬨﬧ, הﬧﬦﬦﬦ ﬧ ﬦﬦﬡﬦﬦ; כﬦ ﬡﬧ הﬧﬧ
וﬦﬨﬡﬧﬧﬦ וﬤﬧﬧﬨ ﬡﬦﬦ וﬦ﬩ﬦﬦ־ ﬦﬦ הﬨﬦﬡﬦ﬩ﬦﬦﬦﬧ; ﬦﬤﬨ חﬧ﬩ וﬦﬧﬨﬦﬨ
גﬦ ﬦﬦﬤﬦ הﬦﬡﬦﬡﬨﬤ, הﬦﬦﬨﬦ﬩ ﬦﬦ ﬦﬡﬧﬦﬨ; וﬦﬦ ﬦﬦﬤﬧﬦ ﬤﬤﬦ
הﬦﬡﬦﬧﬦ ﬦﬦﬧﬦﬨ ﬦﬦﬦﬦ

. וﬦﬦ כﬦ וﬦﬦﬤ ﬦﬦﬤﬤﬦﬨﬦﬨﬦ ﬦﬦ﬩ ﬩ﬦ﬩ﬨﬦ כﬦﬦﬦﬨ ﬦﬦ﬩ﬦﬦ
ﬦﬦﬤﬦﬦﬦﬧ ﬦﬦﬦﬤﬦﬦ וﬦﬤﬧ וﬦ﬩ﬦﬤﬤ ﬤﬤﬦﬦﬦ﬩ﬤ כﬦ ﬦﬧﬧﬤﬧﬨ חﬧﬦﬦﬦﬦ
־ ﬦﬦﬧﬦﬦ ﬦﬦﬤﬤ ﬦﬦﬦﬦﬦﬦﬦ ﬦﬨﬦﬨ ﬦﬦ﬩ ﬦﬦﬦﬨﬦ ﬦﬤﬦﬨﬦﬦ ﬤﬤ
ﬦﬦﬦﬦﬦﬦ ﬦﬧﬤﬨ ﬦﬦﬦﬨ וﬦﬤﬧ ﬦﬦﬧﬦ ﬦﬦﬧﬦ ﬤﬧﬦﬧ ﬤﬦﬨﬧﬧﬤ הﬦﬤﬧﬦﬦ
ﬦﬦﬦﬨ כﬦ ,ﬦﬦﬨﬤﬦ ﬦﬦﬦﬦﬧﬨ ﬦﬦ נה ﬧ﬩ﬧﬧﬤﬨ, ﬧﬦ כﬦ ﬦﬧﬤﬦ
נﬧ כ﬩ﬦﬤﬤﬨ גﬦ הﬦ ﬤﬦ ﬤﬦ הﬦﬦﬦﬤ הﬦﬤ ﬤﬤ' ﬦﬦﬤ
וﬦﬤﬦﬧ ﬦﬦﬤﬦ ﬦﬦﬦﬦ ﬤﬦﬦﬦﬤ. וﬦﬤﬧﬦﬤﬦ ﬦﬦ הﬧﬦﬦﬦﬦﬨ
וﬤﬦ ﬦﬦ' ﬦﬦ.ﬦ. ﬧﬦﬦﬦ ﬦﬤﬤ נה ﬦﬦﬦﬦﬦﬦ ﬧﬧ הﬧﬦﬦﬦﬤﬦﬧ
ﬦﬦﬦ' חﬤﬤﬦ ﬦﬧﬦﬤ גﬦ ﬦﬦﬨ הﬦﬤﬦﬦﬦﬨ ﬦﬧﬦﬦﬤ וﬦﬦﬤﬤﬦﬦ

Number 81   Side Two

עליהם בכל הנהגת התורה והשלוה, אשר מקום חכם צריך
להקוט על זה בלמעה עיניו

ואם מסכימים בקובץ לזה ויסכו גם להודיע לי.
זה בהקדם ואז נדע לקחת על לבינו תיכף את ההוצאה
ולבוא בכתובים עם הרב ז"ל מחיפה.

ויהי' נא מטובם כי מכתבם זה יהי' חתום גם
מראש הבור קירושלים כהרב הגאון ר' חיים ז"ל ברלין
והרב הגאון ר' חיים יוסף ז"ל זאננענפעלד, ואז אשר
נוכל לסמוך על זה בהחלט גמור

האורה לשפת ערבי יהי' כמו כן קודם אל ירא
שמים, אם אם לא נמצא לו במאמת יהי' א"ל נכבדי
הנני כותב בקיצור כי בלא התנאי הזה לא
אוכל להועיל כל מאומה. כי כן התנאי המתנדבים ולא
ירצו לזוז מזה

הנני נשאר פה עד מחרת ר"ח הבע"ל. ועל כן
יהי' נא מטובם לשלוח מכתבם לפה

והנני מכבדם ומוקירם
יצחק אייזיק הלוי

האמבורג א"ו לפה

Rabbiner dr. Kottek
für Rabbiner Halevy in Bad Homburg
Deutschland

Number 81 Side Three

ב"ה יום ו' עש"ק ח' טבת תרס"ט

למעלת כבוד הרב הגאון האמיתי המפורסם כש"ת
הקדוש מוהרר חיים נ"י הגאבד"ק בריסק יע"א

אחדשה"ט, היום קבלתי מפראנקפורט מאסיפתנו הכללית
ומצאתי את מכתב מעכת"ה על העתק מכתבם
לקושטא, וכן מצאתי דעפעשע מקושטא, כי ע"פ הענין
מלכותנו וטוב בעזה"י, ומתרעמים מאד כי עוד לא
באו המכתבים מרוסיא, ומבקשים כי ישלח פסק
קבלת בין מירושלים לקושטא כי איסור גמור הוא
לברור הרב שאינו הגון בחיים נחום
והנני מהר לשנות למעכת"ה ולבאר לו
את כל הדברים האלה.
במכתבם לקושטא טענו חלוב כי חיים
נחום ירצה להיות כמו גידעמאן רב ברוסיא, וגם
טעות הם ובחר חס ושלום הנהו לה רב רבנן
בשם אדונינו ורבינו ובכל מצבו לכל רבני המדינה
עומדים תחתיו והינו ... והעקרים
ומבקשים הם גם פסק קבלת בין מירושלים
על זה הנני אומר אני לכבד עתה
ביחוד, רבני ירושלים אשר הם היו צריכים

Number 88a to Rabbi Haim Soloveichik, 8 Tevet 5669
(Only first side extant)

Number 94 to Rabbi Haim Berlin, 13 Shevat 5669

ב"ה האניווארג יום ג' י"ט סיון תרס"ט

אגלות כבוד הרב הגאון הגדול המפורסם חריף ובקי
קדושי תורה מוהר"ר אליעזר י' גארדאן הגאב"ד
דק"ק טעלז יע"א מרבב שלום

...

אחדשה"ט, ראה. ונהיגי וכו' צ' כאורך אליהנו נענו ודבר
עלינו והתאלם וחד צ"ר יחיהי סגולת הרבנים עדותיה
י' והתואלם יחד קנועג אלרבי הרב אמרנה ועלונו הרב
 והרב צ' ד' אורך, ורבאל ככסו

וקרשו את הרבר לאחר ל' אם ומקאד-צ
הויפמורג הסאובה ואראנפורג

וכהר הסגיחו ואקול קעונה. הגאון הגאיתי הרב
דק"ק קדיסט י', והרב הגאון ד' חיים צאנר י' וואוילנא
והרבני וואקאווסקי י'

והנה לא כתפתי על נה צ"ר עתה ודהד ר'
כי יעדתי כי כאה עלא הנעישה — צ' ירבאהו — וג"ר
והאסיסבה וווילנא לא קא. אך הנה נרצ א. כי יסו
נאתה תקרוב לויסינגעא, ולא כן הנע ומקל קל"ת

תהרינו הוכתפיץ ה'ו וראות כי נין נסיעתו וכיסינגען
תהי מקום כנה אלר יה' תלתפרו וקוה קשנה' והולך
הקום כהינו על לקת נחלו ולים ותלך הותכית
או והלאונבורג אים יותר טום ולנו ולקת כבתלקם
וולקום כל וים והלסיכה והותכיק הסוונכ
העוונכ גדולים והכתפיץ והוה כי קשנה'
וולך טנה תועות גדולה ,ול יה' עונד אל
ונהל או ורעת וראת אות אלר אלר יהולו ויה'
לא טום כתר והוכיע נה כהחונו
תולאו יה' כל הבקר כסור אלכו כתר כי
עד אלר וקוחו הבקריי ועלה או נהכון כי
וורכו טנה כהר
והנו וכתקו ווקודו הוכרכו כל טום
ולתק לעיינו הוו

Rabbiner Halevy Rutschbahn
in Hamburg Deutschland
הָרַבִּי יצחק אי

Number 104   Side Two

כ"ה · ב' סיון תרס"ט

Herrn Jacob Rosenheim נ"י

מרכבה ואלוף חו"ר צב הצולה

[handwritten Hebrew letter text]

Number 105 to Jacob Rosenheim, 20 Sivan 5669

קול ,ואג' ה' ע אצ'ע' כול גאות' וגאות' ל'ו| גה כ' לא| וגב
ולא' כ' אקו וגב התפל? ופ'ו אצ'ע' את וגב הק'ו
הרקה אה'ע

כ' ע'ו כו כל אל' כתור אל'ע' כ'ע'ע' הוע
ע'אה'ע' כאהכה ואחוה, סכנה גכוה ה'א ועירם אות'
הרפה כתוק ע'ע'ע' הכל ה' וחכ'ע' ור'א' כ' וב'
לפ'צ'ו ו' כר' הוא וגב רוח' ורצ'ת' אל' קמ'ו
ה'ע

הכ'ע'כ'ס א'ע'ו הוא וג'ר' ה'כ'ק לק ול'ה כ'
הע'ע' כול ור'א'ו, ה'ע' וכ'ע' אפס ו'ות'ע' וב' פ'הק'ה
אוכ'ות'א' ור'א'ו' הק, ואפ'' את' מ' וש'ו' וס'ר' רק
ע'לכ' אק'ע' ע'ע' אחכ'ע הוא ה'ע'| הנה הוא כ'|
פ'כ'א ול'פ'' א'ע' יה'ו וע'ע' כ'א'כ' וכ'ר' הנה לק ע'
הוא ו'ו'כו כל פ'כ'א|
ו'א'ע לק' יע'ע'רו' כ' וכ'ת'ת' א' ס'גוע'ת' אכ'ק
כ'וס'א, וכ'כ'ר' א' ע' יק'ו קורה אוהה .

בה יום ב' י' אדר תרע"ב

אל עלאת כבוד ידיד נפל' ולמדי הרב הג' המפורסם
נ"ר ומא"ץ וע"ה הרבר המפואר אוהבלו ר' ר'
קוטעק הג'א'פ' דכ'נ הותיקא מרכה ושלום חיי עד עול'

קראתי יקרחן ושמחתי ולאחות ... ...
הנה ידידינו ... ... יוכיר רק לא ...
עוד ... עיקר הכל הדבר קטיתן קבל צדד, ור'
... ... רפואה שלמה ותרכבא לעיני
כל עיני עין עין ...
יתר הדברים כתם קל ר' ...
והנו עלת רק על דבר כדיו הסיפור
כי הא' ... ... קית קיו ... ...
... וכו אבדות ... הגלות והלך ...
חול עלו והכריו ... זכות גיור
והכרוע הנה ... ...
... ... לא יכרב ... הגלותן והוא זכות
גאור, על ... ... ורכון ... על ... קית קיו
והנו ... ...
... ... עים
... ... הי.

Number 145 to Rabbi Heimann Kottek, 10 Adar 5672

Number 152a To Rabbi Heimann Kottek, 15 Heshvan 5673

ויען דקר"

Halevy's Monument

פה נגנז ארון הלוים

הרב הגאון האמתי חוקר האלקי

שר התורה והחכמה נפלאותי

עמוד הימיני מאור ישראל וקדושתו

מחבר הדורות הראשונים

'אדוננו מורנו ורבנו מוהר"ר יצחק אייזיק

הלוי זצ"ל לה"ה ראבינאוויטץ

במוהר"ר אליהו הלוי זצ"ל ממשפחת

האיוועניטצער המפורסמה ברוסיא

שיצאה נשמתו בטהרה בליל ש"ק פ' אמור כ' אייר

לה' לשבי ונקבר באבל כבד כבד ביום א' פ' ב"ב

כ"א אייר תרע"ד

לכל יש תמורה אבל לא ליחיד לעמו אשר גאונות אמתית

בכל רחבי ים התלמוד בבלי וירושלמי וכח אלקי בחקירת

חכמת ישראל יחד בו נפשו חכמת ישראל נתיתמה וכנסת

ישראל אבדה קברניטה ובחיר גאוניה כבר בימי עלומיו

נמנה לגדול התורה ברוסיא ופרי ימי עלומיו הוא הבתים

לבדים על ש"ס עודנו בכתובים להאיר עיני כל ישראל בעומק

למודו הנפלא שהטבע על אדני האמת הברורה בתור חוקר

אלקי לחם מלחמת תנופה נגד מחבלי כרם חכמת ישראל ויאר

אור חדש על ישראל ותורתו בספרו דורות הראשונים

אשר ממנו הותחלו דברי ימי ישראל להכתב וחכמת ישראל

להבנות מימי שחרותו לא עשו גדולי התורה ברוסיא שום דבר

בעניני הכלל בלי עצתו והסכמתו ובן כ"א שנה נתמנה למנהיג

בישיבת וואלאזין אשר ממנה יצאה תורה לכל העולם הוא גם היה

מחולל הרעיון הנשגב של אגודת ישראל ועד יומו האחרון

עמד על משמרתה בתור אחד ממנהיגיה היותר ראשונים

יחסה ויתלונן בצל אלקי ישראל אשר בו בטח והאמין

וינוח ויעמוד לגורלו לקץ הימין

ת' נ' צ' ב' ה'

159

Bibliography

Halevy's Published Writings
(In Chronological Order)

„דברי שלום ואמת״, הלבנון, שנה ט״ז, מספר 28 (13 פברואר 1880), ע׳ 227-279;
מספר 35, ע׳ 273-274; מס׳ 42, ע׳ 329-331. (בלי שמו בחתימה). מאמריו
אלה נדפסו גם בספר דברי שלום ואמת, מאת יעקב ליפשיץ. ווארשא, תרמ״ד.

„קבלת אבות״, בן עמי, ווילנה, אפריל-מאי, 1887. ע׳ 45-60.

„מכתב להעיר״, בספר דברי ימי ישראל מאת צבי גרעטז, חלק שלישי. מתורגם
על ידי שאול פינחס ראבינאוויץ. ווארשא, תרנ״ד. ע׳ 490-492.

"La Cloture du Talmud et Les Saboraim." RdEJ, XXXIII (1896),
pp. 1-17; XXIV (1897), pp. 241-250.

דורות הראשונים. חלק שלישי (מן חתימת התלמוד עד סוף ימי הגאונים).
פרעסבורג, תרנ״ז.

דורות הראשונים. חלק שני (מסוף ימי המשנה עד אחר חתימת התלמוד).
פראנקפורט, תרס״א.

שני מכתבים משנת תרס״ד. בספר מי נתן למשיסה יעקב וישראל לבחזים, מאת
משה חיים אפרים בלאך. ניו יארק, תשי״ז. ע׳ 163-172.

דורות הראשונים. חלק ראשון, כרך שלישי. (מסוף ימי החשמונאים עד ימי
נציבי רומא) פראנקפורט, תרס״ו.

"Nachbemerkung der Redaktion." JdJLG, V (1907), pp. 238-244. (This
article is a translation from the Hebrew by the editors.)

דורות הראשונים. חלק ראשון, כרך חמישי. (מאחר החורבן עד חתימת המשנה)
הובא לדפוס ע״י המחבר עד ע׳ 208 ויתר הספר יצא לאור מכתב היד אשר
הניח אחריו ע״י שלמה מנחם הלוי באמבערגער. פראנקפורט, תרע״ח.

דורות הראשונים. כרך ששי. (תקופת המקרא) עם הערות של שמואל הלוי, והקדמה
מאת י. ל. הכהן פישמן, ודברים אחדים מאת ב. מ. לוין. ירושלים: מוסד
הרב קוק, תרצ״ט.

„משקלקלו הכותים״, עם הערות של משה אויערבך. ספר היובל ה-25 של „בית
יעקב״ בתל-אביב. תל-אביב, תשכ״א, ע׳ קלב-ג.

דורות הראשונים. חלק ראשון, כרך רביעי. (התקופה האחרונה של הבית השני, זמן
נציבי רומא והמלחמה) מעובד ע״י משה אויערבך. בני ברק: נצח, תשכ״ד.

קטעים מכתביו בספר זכרון לרבי יצחק אייזיק הלוי, נערך ממשה אויערבך.
בני ברק: נצח, תשכ״ד. ע׳ כ׳-כ״א, ל״ה, מ״ז, נ״ד, נ״ה-נ״ח, ס׳-ס״ב, צ״א-צ״ב.

Encyclopedic Works Which List Halevy

HEBREW AND YIDDISH

אייזענשטאט, בן ציון, דור רבניו וסופריו. ספר ששי. ניו יארק, תרס"ה. ע' 28.
האנציקלופדיה העברית. חלק י"ד. ירושלים, תשכ"ב. ע' 468.
הלחמי, דוד, חכמי ישראל — אנצקלופדיה לגדולי ישראל בדורות האחרונים.
תל־אביב: אברהם ציוני, תשי"ח. ע' ש"ע.
פינס, דן, אנציקלופדיה לעם. תל־אביב: עמיחי, תשי"ג. ע' 537.
פיעטרושקא, ש., יידישע פֿאָלקס־ענציקלאָפּעדיע. ערשטע באנד. מאנטרעאל,
שפּאלט 731. 1943.
קרסל, ג., לכסיקון הספרות העברית בדורות האחרונים. כרך שני. רחביה,
תשכ"ז. ע' 819.

ENGLISH, GERMAN AND RUSSIAN

Encyclopedia Judaica, Vol. VII. Berlin: Eshkol, 1931. P. 867.

Grosse Juedische National-Biographie, Vol. VII. 1936. P. 500.

Juedisches Lexikon, Vol. II. Berlin: Juedischer Verlag, 1928. P. 1360.

Standard Jewish Encyclopedia. Jerusalem-Tel-Aviv: Massadah, 1958/9.
P. 826.

Universal Jewish Encyclopedia, Vol. V. New York, 1941. P. 178.

Vallentine's Jewish Encyclopedia. London: Shapiro, Vallentine & Co.,
1938. P. 263.

Yevreiskaya Enziklopedia, Vol. VI. Petersburg, 1910. P. 58.

Biographical

HEBREW AND YIDDISH

ספר זכרון לרבי יצחק אייזיק הלוי, בעריכת משה אויערבך. בני ברק: נצח,
תשכ"ד.
אבידור, שמואל, "ליובל ה־50 של 'ועידת קטוביץ' ". פנים אל פנים, ירושלים,
מספר 164, י"ג סיון, תשכ"ב, ע' 10 ולה'.
אליאש, מרדכי, "ר' זאב יעבץ". אישים ודמויות בחכמת ישראל באירופה המזרחית
לפני שקיעתה, בעריכת שמואל ק. מירסקי, עוגן, תשי"ט. ע' 155־173.
—————— ר' יצחק אייזיק הלוי (רבינוביץ)". בספר הנ"ל. ע' 65־115.
—————— "אבן מאסו הבונים היתה לראש פנה". ספר זכרון לרבי יצחק אייזיק
הלוי. ע' קל"א־קמ"א.
אראן, ווילי, "אינטערעסאנטע פאסירונגען און שיינע פערזענליכקייטן פון מיין
היים־שטאט האמבורג אין דייטשלאנד". דער טאג, ניו יארק, 8טען אפריל,
1944, זייט 5.

Biographical (Continued)

בלויא, משה, על חומותיך ירושלים. תל־אביב: נצח, תש"ו.

ברלין, מאיר, פון וואלאזין ביז ירושלים. ניו יארק, תרצ"ז.

גלייכער, מ. י., „רבי יצחק אייזיק הלוי". קול ישראל, ירושלים, ט"ו אייר תש"ו, ע' 2.

דוקעס, יחזקאל, אוה למושב. קראקא, תרס"ג. ע' 140.

הדרך, פרנקפורט, תמוז, תרע"ד, ע' 1.

היינמן, יצחק, „ר' מרדכי הלוי הורביץ ותפיסת היהדות שלו", סיני, ירושלים, שנה ז', חוברת ח"ט (טבת־שבט, תש"ד), ע' קס"ב־קע"א.

הלוי, שמואל, „אבי זכרונו לברכה". ספר זכרון לרבי יצחק אייזיק הלוי. ע' י"ג־ס"ג. טאג־מארגען זשורנאל, ניו יארק, 20טער נאוועמבער, 1959. זייט 14.

יעקבזון, בנימין זאב, זכרונות. ירושלים: מרכז לספרות חרדית בא"י, תשי"ג.

לוין, בנימין מ., „דברים אחדים". דורות הראשונים. כרך ששי. יצחק אייזיק הלוי. ירושלים: מוסד הרב קוק, תרצ"ט. ע' ט'־י'.

——— „מתולדותי", סיני, ירושלים, שנה ז', חוברת י־י"א (אדר־ניסן, תש"ד) ע' קצ"ו.

ליפשיץ, יעקב, זכרון יעקב. חלק ראשון. קאוונא־סלאבאדקא, 1924; חלק שלישי. קובנה, 1930.

מארקוס, שלמה, „למותו של הגאון בעל 'דורות הראשונים'". הצפירה, ורשה, שנה 40, גליון ק"ו (כ"ה אייר, תרע"ד), ע' 2.

מגיד, הלל נח, עיר ווילנא. ווילנא: ראם, תר"ס.

מירסקי, שמואל קלמן, „על חכמת ישראל במזרח אירופה". אישים ודמויות בחכמת ישראל, בעריכתו, עוגן, תשי"ט. ע' 5 עד 64.

מכתבי ברכה והסכמה מאת גדולי דורנו שלא הספיקו לבא אל האספה בקטוביץ. פרנקפורט, תרע"ג.

העברי, ברלין, שנה ג' 1912.

פישמן, י. ל., „הקדמה". דורות הראשונים. כרך ששי. יצחק אייזיק הלוי. ירושלים: מוסד הרב קוק, תרצ"ט ע' ג'־ח'.

פרידענזאן, יוסף, „דער היסטאַרישער וועג פון אגודת ישראל". דאס אידישע וואָרט, ניו יארק, ערשטער יארגאנג, נומער 7 (סיון, תשי"ד), זייטען 18־24.

הצפירה, ורשה, שנה 40, גליון ק"ז (כ"ב אייר, תרע"ד), ע' 3.

קוק, אברהם יצחק, אגרות הראיה. ירושלים: מוסד הרב קוק, תש"ג.

——— „הגאון ר' י"א הלוי". מוריה, שנה ה' גליון 537 (תרע"ד).

קפלן, צבי, „בעל 'דורות הראשונים'". הצופה, כ"א תשרי תשכ"ה, ע' 3־4.

ראבינאוויץ, אליהו עקיבא, „חבל על דאבדין". המודיע, פאלטאווע, שנה ה', מספר 30 (כ"ו אייר, תרע"ד), ע' 466־468.

רוזנהיים, יעקב, זכרונות. תל־אביב: שערים, תשט"ז.

——— קול יעקב. תל־אביב: נצח, תשי"ד.

Biographical (Continued)

רייכ"ל, אשר, "די בריק צווישען מזרח און מעריב". דאס אידישע ווארט, חשון,
תשכ"א, זייט 11.

—————— "דער מייסטער־ארכיטעקט פון אגודת ישראל". דאס אידישע ווארט,
חשון, תשכ"ג, זייטען 98־99.

—————— "הרב יצחק אייזיק הלוי". דגלנו, תל־אביב: אב, תשכ"ג, ע' ב.

—————— "ההיסטוריון החרדי". ספר זכרון לרבי יצחק אייזיק הלוי. ע'
קמ"ב־קנ"א.

שנפלד, משה, ורוטנברג, יחזקאל, מקטוביץ עד ירושלים אגודת ישראל בתמונות
ומסמכים. תל־אביב: נצח, תשי"ד.

שרביט, י., "ביבליוגרפיה (בלתי מושלמת)". ספר זכרון לרבי יצחק אייזיק הלוי.
ע' פ.

English and German

Agudas Jisroel Berichte und Materialien herausgegeben vom Provisorischen Comite de "Agudas Jisroel" zu Frankfurt a. M. (1912).

Aron, William, *Jews of Hamburg.* New York, 1967. Pp. 52-55.

Beilage zur *Allgemeine Zeitung des Judentums,* Der Gemeindebote, Berlin, LXXVIII, No. 22 (May 29, 1914), p. 3.

American Jewish Year Book 5675. Philadelphia: Jewish Publication Society, 1914. P. 195.

Frankfurter Israelitisches Familienblatt, XII, No. 20 (May 22, 1914), p. 1.

Die Freie Vereinigung fuer die Interessen des orthodoxen Judentums und Erez Jisroel. Folge I. Frankfurt: Hermon, 1935.

Freie Vereinigung fuer die Interessen des orthodoxen Judentums Mitteilungen an die Vereinsmitglieder. No. 20. Frankfurt, 1908.

Grunfeld, Isidor, *Three Generations.* London: Jewish Post, 1958.

Haderech. Nachrichten des Deutschen Gruppenverbandes und der Jugendorganisation der Agudas Jisroel. Berlin, Nr. 4, June, 1914.

Der Israelit, Frankfurt, "Erinnerungen an Isaak Halevy." LV, No. 23 (June 4, 1914), pp. 2-4.

—————— "Isaac Halevy." LV, No. 21 (May 21, 1914), p. 3.

—————— "Personalien-Rabbiner Dr. Heimann Kottek." LIV, No. 1 (January 2, 1913), pp. 9-10.

—————— "Rabbi Jizchok Halevy." LXX, Nrs. 21-23, May 23, 30 and June 6, 1929, pp. 1ff., respectively.

—————— "Vereinswesen." LV, No. 28 (July 9, 1914), p. 9.

Biographical (Continued)

Israelitisches Familienblatt, Hamburg, May 28, 1914, p. 3.

Israelitisches Wochenblatt, Berlin. "Aus den Gemeinden." XIII, No. 22 (May 29, 1914), p. 344; No. 25 (June 19, 1914), p. 389.

Reichel, Oscar Asher, *The Life and Letters of Isaac Halevy* (1847-1914). Dissertation. New York: Bernard Revel Graduate School, Yeshiva University, 1960.

———————— "Isaac Halevy — Architect of Agudath Israel." *Jewish Life,* New York, February, 1962, pp. 41-47.

Rosenheim, Jacob, *Ohole Yaakov — Ausgewahlte Aufsatze und Ansprachen.* Vol. II. Frankfurt: J. Kauffman, 1930. Pp. 469-472.

———————— *Erinnerungen.* In manuscript.

Schwab, Hermann, *Chachme Ashkenaz.* London: Mitre, 1964.

———————— *History of Orthodox Jewry in Germany.* London, 1950.

———————— *A World in Ruins.* London, 1946.

Zweiter Rechenschafts-Bericht der Juedisch-Literarischen Gesellschaft fuer die Jahre 1904-1906. Frankfurt, 1907.

Reviews of the Dorot Harishonim

HEBREW

אטלס, אליעזר, „אור וצל בתולדות ישראל". ספר השנה של נחום סאקאלאוו. שנה א'. תר"ס. ע' 102־124.

אליאש, מרדכי, „ר' יצחק אייזיק הלוי (רבינוביץ)". אישים ודמויות בחכמת ישראל, בעריכת שמואל קלמן מירסקי. עוגן, תשי"ט. ע' 65 עד 115.

וינברג, יחיאל י., „על דרכו של רי"א הלוי בחקר המשנה". סיני, שנה כ"ג, כרך מ"ו (טבת, תש"ד), ע' רכ"ב־ר"ל.

———— „שיטת רי"א הלוי בחקר המשנה". סורא, ירושלים, תשכ"ד. ע' 105־136.

נאכט, יעקב, „דורות הראשונים". המליץ. פטרבורג. שנת ל"ח, מספר 57 (כ"ח אדר תרנ"ח) ע' 6־7.

עפשטיין, אברהם, „אגרות בקורת — ר' יצחק הלוי בעל ס' דורות הראשונים". האשכול, כרך ה', תרס"ה, ע' 256־259. מאמר זה נמצא גם בספר כתבי ר' אברהם עפשטיין. כרך שני. ירושלים: מוסד הרב קוק, תשי"ג. עמודים שנ"ד־שנ"ח.

צינוביץ, מ., „בעל 'דורות הראשונים' ". הצופה, ד' סיון תשכ"ד, ע' 4.

Reviews of the Dorot Harishonim (Continued)

ראטנער, בער, „טעות סופרים". המליץ, פטרבורג, שנה 39, תר"ס. עי' לוח
מפתחות שם.

—————— „והנקרנים תופשין אותי על כך!" המליץ, שנה 40, תרס"א. לוח
מפתחות שם.

שמחוני, י. נ., „דורות הראשונים". התקופה, שנה 11, תרפ"א, ע' 427-444; שנות
14-15, תרפ"ב, ע' 577-606.

ENGLISH, FRENCH, GERMAN AND HUNGARIAN

J.M.B., "Halevy's Wissenschaftliche Methode." *Der Israelit,* LVI, No. 19
(April 29, 1915), p. 3; No. 20 (May 6, 1915), p. 2.

Bacher, Wilhelm, A Review of Vol. II. *REJ,* XLIV (1902), pp. 132-151.

Blau, Lajos, *Magyar Zsido Szemle.* 1900-1903, 1907, 1915.

Bondi, Jonas, *"Ein Neuer Band Halevy."* *Der Israelit,* XLVII, No. 32
(August 9, 1906), p. 10.

—————— "Simon der Gerechte. Eine Richtigstellung nach Halevys
Doroth Harischonim." *JdJLG,* V (1907), pp. 245-277.

—————— "Der Juedische Krieg gegen Hadrian nach dem Dorot
Harischonim." *JdJLG,* XIII (1920), pp. 255-280.

Breuer, Joseph, "Zum Doroth Harischonim (Teil Ie)." *Juedischen
Monatshefte,* VII (1920), pp. 159-166.

Elbogen, Ismar, "Die Neuste Construction der juedischen Geschichte."
MGWJ, XLVI (1902), pp. 1-48.

Epstein, Abraham, "Les Saboraim." *REJ,* XXXVI (1898), pp. 222-236.

—————— "Le Retour de Rab en Babylonie d'Apres M. Isaac Halevy."
REJ, XLIV (1902), pp. 45-62.

—————— "Ordination et Autorisation." *REJ, XLVI* (1903) pp.
197-211.

Frankl, Philipp, "Der Erste Teil (3. Band) des 'Doroth Horischonim'
v. Halevy." *Frankfurter Israelitisches Familienblatt,* IV, No. 46
(November 30, 1906), p. 1.

Halevy, Samuel, "Ist der Name 'Juedischer Hellenismus' berechtigt?"
JdJLG, IX (1911), pp. 421-489.

—————— "Uebersetzungsprobe zu Dorot Harischonim." *JdJLG,* XVII
(1926), pp. 163-186.

Herzog, Jacob David, *The Mishnah Berakoth Peah Demai* — Translation
Introduction and New Commentary. Jerusalem, 1945. Pp. VIII-XI,
XXIII-XXVI.

Reviews of the Dorot Harishonim (Continued)

Hoffmann, David, "Bemerkungen zur Geschichte des Synedrion." *JdJLG*,
   V (1907), pp. 225-238.

————— "Ein Meisterwerk." (A review of Vol. III). *Israelitische
Monatsschrift — Wissenschaftliche Beilage zur Juedischen Presse,*
VII, No. 33 (August 15, 1901).

————— A Review of Vol. II. *ZfHB, V* (1901), pp. 100-107.

Jawitz, Wolf, "Neue juedische Geschichtsforschung und einige ihrer
   wichtigsten Resultate." *JdJLG*, IV (1906), pp. 283-292.

Kottek, Heimann, "Der Kaiser Diokletian in Palestina." *JdJLG*, I (1903),
   pp. 213-223.

————— "Bachers Besprechung des Doroth Harischonim II." *JdJLG*,
II (1904), pp. 85-184.

————— *Fortschritt oder Rueckschritt in der Juedischen Wissenschaft.*
1904. Reprint of *loc. cit.*

————— "Die Hochschulen in Palestina and Babylonien." *JdJLG*,
III (1905), pp. 131-190.

Kronberg, N., "Die Amoraer in neuer Beleuchtung." *MGWJ*, XLVI
   (1902), pp. 439-448.

Lange, Gerson, "Die Kabaloth und Drashot, das Verhaeltnis zwischen
   Ueberlieferung und Deutung der Schrift nach Halevy." *Unser Weg,*
   VI (1920), pp. 179-193; VI (1921), pp. 1-8, 35-47.

Leszynsky, Rudolf, "Isak Halevis Zitate." *MGWJ*, LVI (1912), pp.
   567-580, 690-699.

Levy, Israel, A Review of Vol. II. *REJ*, XLIII (1901), pp. 279-280.

Marcus, Ahron, "Doroth Harischonim." *Frankfurter Israelitisches
Familienblatt,* V, No. 16 (April 26, 1907), p. 9; No. 19, p. 9;
No. 22, p. 9; No. 29, p. 9; No. 31, p. 9; No. 35, p. 9.

————— "Buecherschau." *Krakauer Juedische Zeitung,* Jan. 13, 1899,
   pp. 6-9; Feb. 13, pp. 2-5; April, pp. 10-12; May, pp. 3-4.

Marx, A., A Review of Vol. II. *ZfHB*, VI (1902), pp. 134-136.

Nacht, Albert, *Einst und Jetzt in der Juedischen Wissenschaft.* Frankfurt:
   Kauffmann, 1899. (Gegen Epstein's Recension des Halevy'sche
   Werkes D.H. Teil III.)

Unna, Isak, "Babylonien um das Ende der Tannaitenzeit." *JdJLG*, I
   (1903), pp. 269-277.

Waxman, Meyer, *A History of Jewish Literature.* Vol. IV. New York:
   Bloch, 1941. Pp. 720-727.

Other Works Referring to the Dorot Harishonim

Hebrew and Yiddish

אויערבאך, משה, תולדות עם ישראל. ד׳ חלקים. ירושלים: המרכז לספרות חרדית בא״י, תש״ח-תש״ט.

אלבק, חנוך, "ביקורת או עקשות". סיני, שנה כ״ג, כרך מ״ו (טבת, תש״ך), ע׳ רל״ה-רנ״ח.

————— מבוא למשנה. ירושלים: מוסד ביאליק, תשי״ט.

————— ששה סדרי משנה — סדר מועד. ירושלים-תל-אביב, תשי״ט.

אלון, גדליהו, תולדות היהודים בארץ ישראל בתקופת המשנה והתלמוד. הקיבוץ המאוחד, תשי״ג.

————— מחקרים בתולדות ישראל. כרך ראשון. תל-אביב: הקיבוץ המאוחד, תשי״ז.

אנציקלופדיה תלמודית. כרך תשיעי. ירושלים, תשי״ט.

אסף, שמחה, תקופת הגאונים וספרותה. ירושלים: מוסד הרב קוק, תשט״ו. ע׳ קנ״ט, ק״ס, קס״ח, ר״ל, רע״א.

אפשטיין, יעקב נחום, מבואות לספרות התנאים. תל-אביב, 1957.

בעהר, משלם פישל, דברי משלם. פראנקפורט, תרפ״ו. ע׳ 81-61.

גדנסקי, א. א. "טעות סופר". ישורון, תל-אביב, גליון ד׳ (כ״ב אב תש״ח), ע׳ 7.

גוטקבסקי, יעקב, קורות עם עולם. ד׳ חלקים. לאדז: מסורה, תרצ״ג-תרצ״ה.

היימאן, אהרן, אגרת דרבינו שרירא גאון. לונדון, תר״ע.

————— תולדות תנאים ואמוראים. ג׳ חלקים. לונדון, תר״ע.

וויינברג, יחיאל יעקב, "לחקר המשנה". ספר היובל לכבוד שמואל קלמן מירסקי. ניו יורק, תשי״ח.

————— "דרכו של רי״א הלוי ושיטתו בחקר המשנה". תלפיות, ניו-יורק, ניסן, תשכ״ה. ע׳ 38-48.

וויס, אברהם, התהוות התלמוד בשלמותו. ניו יארק, תש״ג.

————— "לשאלת מקורות הסוגיות". הצפה לחכמת ישראל, ט׳ (1925), ע׳ 177 ול׳.

זילבער, אברהם, הדורות מראש. ניו יארק: סיני, תשי״ט.

זלוטניק, ישעיהו, "הכרונולוגיה של התלמוד והבנת התלמוד". הצופה לחכמת ישראל, בודאפעסט. שנה י״ב, חוב׳ א׳, תרפ״ח. ע׳ 48, 319.

חורגין, פנחס, מחקרים בתקופת בית שני. ניו יארק: חורב, תש״י.

טביומי (גוטנטג), טובי׳ יהודא, טל אורות. תל-אביב, תש״ח.

————— טל לישראל. חלק ראשון. פיעטרקוב, תרפ״ו.

טיקוצינסקי, חיים, תקנות הגאונים. מתורגם ע״י מאיר חבצלת. תל-אביב-ירושלים: סורא תש״ך.

טשרנוביץ חיים, תולדות ההלכה. כרך ראשון, חלק ראשון וחלק שני. ניו יארק, תרצ״ה-תרצ״ו.

Other Works Referring to the Dorot Harishonim (Continued)

יעבץ, זאב, תולדות ישראל. חלק׳ ו׳ ז׳ ח׳. מהדורה שלישית. תל־אביב: אחיעבר,
תרצ״ד-תרצ״ח; חלק ט׳. ירושלים, תרצ״ח; חלק י׳. תל־אביב: אחיעבר,
תרצ״ב.

כהנא, קלמן, חקר ועיון, תל־אביב, תש״ך.

כ״ץ, בן ציון, פרושים, צדוקים, קנאים נוצרים. תל־אביב: נ. טברסקי, תש״ה.

לוי, אליעזר, יסודות ההלכה. תל־אביב: סיני, תשי״ג.

לוין, בנימין מנשה, אגרת רב שרירא גאון. חיפה, תרפ״א.

—————— אוצר הגאונים. כרך א׳. חיפה, תרפ״ח; כרכים ב׳-י״ב. ירושלים,
תר״ץ-תש״ג.

—————— מתיבות. ירושלים, תרצ״ד.

—————— רבנן סבוראי ותלמודם. ירושלים: אחיעבר, תרצ״ז.

ליברמן, שאול, תוספת ראשונים. ירושלים: במברגר את וואהרמן, תרצ״ז.

ליפשיץ, יהודא, דור ישרים. חלק ראשון. פיעטרקוב, תרס״ח.

מירסקי, שמואל קלמן, ״על חכמת ישראל במזרח אירופה״. אישים ודמויות
בחכמת ישראל, ערך ש. ק. מירסקי. ע׳ 5 עד 64.

—————— שאילתות דרב אחאי גאון עם ביאורים והערות ומבוא. ירושלים:
המכון למחקר ולהוצאת ספרים סורא וישיבה אוניברסיטה, תש״ך.

מלמד, ע״צ, מבוא לספרות התלמוד. ירושלים: קרית ספר, תשי״ד.

מרגליות, מרדכי, מבואות והערות להלכות הנגיד לר׳ שמואל הנגיד. ירושלים,
תשכ״ב.

מרגליות, ראובן, ״ציונים ביבליוגראפיים״. ארשת, בעריכת נפתלי בן־מנחם
ויצחק רפאל. ירושלים: מוסד הרב קוק, תשי״ט. ע׳ 427.

נויבואר, יקותיאל יעקב, הרמב״ם על דברי סופרים. ירושלים: מוסד הרב קוק,
תשי״ז. ע׳ 155-158.

עמנואל, יונה, ״ספר זכרון על רבי יצחק אייזיק הלוי״. המעין, ירושלים, ניסן,
תשכ״ה, ע׳ 76-80.

פדרבוש, שמעון, בנתיבות התלמוד. ירושלים: מוסד הרב קוק, תשי״ז.

פינקעלשטין, אליעזר א׳, הפרושים ואנשי כנסת הגדולה. ניו יורק, תש״י.

פרשל, טוביה, ״שנתון החברה הספרותית היהודית 1903-1932״. חכמת ישראל
במערב אירופה. כרך שני. ירושלים-ת״א: עוגן, תשכ״ג. ע׳ 348-359.

צורי, יעקב שמואל, תולדות המשפט הצבורי העברי. כרך ראשון, ספר שלישי,
חלק ראשון. לונדון, תרצ״ג.

צייטלין, שניאור זלמן, הצדוקים והפרושים. ניו יארק: חורב, תרצ״ו.

—————— ״שמעון הצדיק וכנסת הגדולה״. נר מערבי. כרך שני. ערך חיים קפלן.
ניו יורק: ישיבת ר׳ יצחק אלחנן, תרפ״ה. ע׳ 137-142.

קאטעק, שמואל הילמן, די יודישע געשיכטע. ווארשא: יודישע ליטעראטור, תרצ״ב.

קלוזנר, יוסף, היסטוריה של הבית השני. כרכ׳ א׳-ה. ירושלים: אחיאסף, תשי״ט.

Other Works Referring to the Dorot Harishonim (Continued)

ראטענבערג, שלמה הכהן, תולדות עם עולם. כרך א. ברוקלין: קרן אליעזר, תשכ"ז.

רבינוביץ, זכריה, „ר' יצחק אייזיק הלוי ומלחמתו ב'בקורת המקרא' ". בית יעקב,
אייר תשכ"ד, ע' 4־5.

רוזנברג, בצלאל, מחשבת בצלאל. ליעדז, תרפ"ו. ע' 27־62.

רייכער, ישעיה, תורת הראשונים. ורשה: ישרון, תרפ"ו.

שליט, אברהם, הורדוס המלך האיש ופעלו. ירושלים: מוסד ביאליק, 1960.

שצרנסקי, מאיר, העבר הישראלי. כרך א. תל־אביב: בית יעקב, תש"ו.

English and German

Albeck, Chanoch, *Untersuchung ueber die Redaktion der Mischna.* Berlin, 1923.

Auerbach, Moses, "Zur Politischen Geschichte der Juden unter Kaiser Hadrian." *Jeschurun,* X (1923), pp. 398-418.

The Babylonian Talmud — Translation into English with Notes. London: Soncino, 1936 *et seq.*

Bamberger, Salomon, "Sadducaer und Pharisaer in ihren Beziehungen zu Alexander Jannai und Salome." *Zweiter Rechenschafts-Bericht der Juedisch-Literarischen Gesellschaft fuer die Jahre 1904-1906,* Frankfurt, 1907. Pp. 3-26.

Belkin, Samuel, *Philo and the Oral Law.* Cambridge: Harvard University, 1940.

Biberfeld, Philip, *Universal Jewish History.* Vol. I. New York: Spero Foundation, 1948. Vol. II. New York: Feldheim, 1962.

Breuer, Joseph, "Juedische Geschichte." *Juedischen Monatshefte,* II (1915), pp. 110 ff., 199-222.

Carlebach, Joseph, "Kritische Rundschau." *Jeschurun,* X (1923), pp. 398-418.

Elbogen, Ismar, "Wie steht es um die zwei Rezensionen des Scherira-Briefes?" *Festschrift zum 75 Jaehrigen bestehen des Juedisch-Theologischen Seminars Fraenckelscher Stiftung.* Vol. 2. Breslau, 1929. Pp. 61-84.

Frank, Edgar, *Talmudic and Rabbinical Chronology.* New York: Feldheim, 1956. P. 31.

Other Works Referring to the Dorot Harishonim (Continued)

Frankl, Philipp, "Das neue Jahrbuch der Juedisch-Literarischen Gesellschaft." *Der Israelit,* XLVIII, No. 33 (August 15, 1907), pp. 11-12.

———— "Jahrbuch der Juedisch-Literarischen Gesellschaft." *Frankfurter Israelitisches Familienblatt,* Feb. 26, 1904, pp. 1-2.

Funk, Salomon, "Raba." *JdLG,* IV (1906), pp. 204-213.

Herford, R. Travers, *The Pharisees.* New York: Macmillan, 1924.

Hoenig, Sidney B., *The Great Sanhedrin.* Philadelphia: Dropsie, 1953.

"Der letzte Talmudheros der Reform." *Der Israelit,* XLVIII, No. 50 (December 12, 1907), p. 2.

K., "Das III. Jahrbuch der 'Juedisch-Literarischen Gesellschaft.'" *Der Israelit,* XLVII, No. 30 (July 26, 1906), pp. 9-10.

Kaplan, Julius, *The Redaction of the Babylonian Talmud.* New York: Bloch, 1933.

Klausner, Joseph, *Jesus of Nazareth.* New York: Macmillan, 1925.

Kottek, Heimann, *Geschichte der Juden.* Frankfurt: Juedisch-Literarische Gesellschaft, 1915.

Lauterbach, Jacob Z., *Midrash and Mishnah.* New York: Bloch, 1916.

Lewin, B., "Zur Charakteristik und Biographie des R. Scherira Gaon." *JdJLG,* VIII (1910), pp. 318-354.

Moore, George Foot, *Judaism in the First Centuries of the Christian Era.* Cambridge: Harvard University, 1927.

Neuwirth, A., "Die deutsche Orthodoxie und die Juedische Geschichtsforschung." *Der Israelit,* LV, No. 26 (June 25, 1914), pp. 3-5.

Reichel, O. Asher, "Isaac Halevy — Orthodox Jewish Historian." *Tradition.* New York, Spring 1963, pp. 247-255.

Schachter, Jacob, *The Student's Guide Through the Talmud by the Eminent Teacher Z. H. Chajes.* New York: Feldheim, 1960.

Stern, Tibor H., *Composition of the Talmud.* New York: 1959.

Strack, Hermann L., *Introduction to the Talmud and Midrash.* Philadelphia: Jewish Publication Society, 1945.

Index